Christian Maturity

Christian Maturity

by Rick C. Howard

*Developed in Cooperation With
the ICI International Office Staff*

ICI
6300 North Belt Line Road
Irving, Texas 75063
USA

First Edition 1978
Second Edition 1980
        Reprinted 1982, 1985, 1988, 1990, 1991, 1993 2/93 3M EP

TO BE USED WITH:
        Student Report Second Edition

S1111E-92

ISBN 1-56390-022-X

Table of Contents

THE ICI CHRISTIAN SERVICE PROGRAM

This independent study textbook is one of 18 courses (subjects) that make up the ICI Christian Service Program. The symbol at the left is a guide for sequenced study. The Christian Service Program is divided into three units of six courses each. *Christian Maturity* is Course One in Unit One.

You may study this course by itself or study the entire series in proper sequence.

Study materials in the Christian Service Program are designed in a self-teaching format for Christian workers. This program will provide a student with the necessary Bible knowledge and skills for practical Christian service. These courses have been especially prepared for Christian workers in all nations and cultures.

ATTENTION

Please read the preliminary instructions for this course very carefully. By following the instructions you should be able to achieve your goals for the course, and you should not have difficulty preparing for your unit student reports.

Address all correspondence concerning the course to your ICI instructor at the address stamped below. In case there is none, and you do not have the address of the ICI office in your area, then please write to the following address:

International Correspondence Institute
6300 North Belt Line Road
Irving, Texas 75063
USA

The address of your local ICI office is:

Course Introduction

Christian maturity is an ever-present goal for believers in Christ. This goal is to reach "the very height of Christ's full stature" (Ephesians 4:13). Although no believer can reach total Christlikeness during earthly life, the Bible places it as the goal for every Christian. It is better to reach for a goal that is too high and gain much than to actually reach a goal that is too low and gain little. The very nature of the subject demands that this course be solidly based on the Bible. Constant reference to Scripture is made throughout the course.

The first part of the course presents *illustrations* of growth, emphasizing the growth of Jesus. Included also are descriptions of natural growth to illustrate spiritual growth. There is comment on hindrances and helps to spiritual advancement. Then, the course centers on *progress* in spiritual growth. Since maturing in Christ is a lengthy process, an effort is made to separate present goals for the believer from the more difficult goals for his future. It is emphasized that our progress includes cooperation with the Holy Spirit and sharing faith with others. Finally, *proofs* of Christian maturity are stressed. Increasing Christlikeness of the believer's character and ministry are presented as evidences of spiritual growth, and the course ends with an emphasis on the transformation of the believer by the Holy Spirit.

The main purpose of the course is to help the student himself become more like Christ, and to encourage him to help others do the same thing. May the Lord bless you and help you to make progress toward maturity in Christ through the study of this course.

Course Description

Christian Maturity is an introductory study to the subject of the Christian's growth. The study gives attention to the role of Christian service in the believer's growth.

A biblical approach to the subject makes the course acceptable for use in an international audience. The course leads the student to constantly interact with the Word of God, which is the foundation for the study.

The course is practical in nature, pointing out how the student may progress toward Christlikeness in daily Christian living and service. Biblical illustrations of Christian growth and the Bible-centered lessons provide the student with material for use in his own Christian service.

Course Objectives

When you finish this course you should be able to:

1. Explain the tendency toward growth inherent in spiritual life, and allow it to help you grow in Christ.

2. Relate spiritual maturity to daily life in such matters as discrimination between good and evil, and application of biblical messages.

3. Explain why a Christian cannot mature without fellowship with God.

4. Explain spiritual maturity in terms of completion and finishing as opposed to flawless perfection.

5. Describe the Holy Spirit's role in our Christian maturity.

6. Explain personal experiences to analyze progress in the use of your will to improve yourself spiritually.

7. Experience greater Christian maturity through increased general usefulness in ministry in the church and in helping others.

Textbooks

You will use *Christian Maturity*: *An Independent Study Textbook* by Rick Howard as both the textbook and study guide for the course. The Bible (*Today's English Version*) is the only other requirement.

Study Time

How much time you actually need to study each lesson depends in part on your knowledge of the subject and the strength of your study skills before you begin the course. The time you spend also depends on the extent to which you follow directions and develop skills necessary for independent study. So plan your study schedule and time, so that you spend enough time to attain the objectives stated by the author of the course and your personal objectives as well.

Units of Study

The lessons in this course are organized into three units of study as follows:

Units	Unit Titles	Lessons
1	Pictures of Christian Maturity	1-4
2	Progress in Christian Maturity	5-7
3	Proofs of Christian Maturity	8-10

Lesson Organization and Study Pattern

Each lesson includes: 1) lesson title, 2) introduction, 3) lesson outline, 4) lesson objectives, 5) learning activities, 6) key words, 7) lesson development including study questions, 8) self-test (at the end of the lesson development) and, 9) answers to each self-test at the back of your textbook.

The lesson outline and objectives will give you an overview of the subject, help you to focus your attention on the most important points as you study, and tell you what you should learn.

The lesson development in this course makes it easy to study the material thoroughly. By studying a section at a time you can make good use of short periods of study whenever you have time, instead of waiting until you have time to do an entire lesson at once. The comments, exercises, and answers are all designed to help you achieve the objectives of the lesson.

Some of the study questions in the lesson development can be answered in the spaces provided in your independent study textbook. But some of the questions require a notebook. As you write the answers in your notebook be sure to record the number and title of the lesson. Write the answers to the study questions in correct numerical order. This will help you in your review for the unit student report.

Do not look ahead at the answers until you have given your answer first. If you give your own answers, you will retain what you study much better. After you have answered the study questions, confirm your answers with the answers given in the textbook. Mark in your notebook the questions you miss and write in the correct answer.

These questions are very important. They will help you develop and improve your knowledge and Christian service. The suggested activities, too, are to help you go from theory to practice.

Ways to Study This Course

If you study this ICI course by yourself, all of your work can be completed by mail. Although ICI has designed this course for you to study on your own, you may also study it in a group or class.

If you study this course in a group or class, the instructor may give you added instructions besides those in the course. If so, be sure to follow his instructions.

Possibly you are interested in using the course in a home Bible study group, in a class at church, or in a Bible school. You will find both the subject content and study methods excellent for these purposes. This course can be helpful to students and teachers alike.

Unit Student Reports

If you are studying independently with ICI, you have received with this course an envelope containing your unit student reports. If you are studying with a group or in a class, you probably received one as well. These are to be completed according to the instructions included in the course and in the instructions in the unit student reports. You should complete and send each unit report to your instructor for his corrections and suggestions regarding your work. Send one when you complete each unit.

Certificate

Upon the successful completion of the course and the final grading of the unit student reports by your ICI instructor, you will receive your Certificate of Award. Or, if you prefer, you may study this course for personal enrichment without receiving a certificate.

Final Examination for Degree Credit

You may earn one unit of degree credit by successful completion of a final examination. You must enroll in the course specifically for credit by submitting a Subject Enrollment Card to your ICI Director. Your Unit Student Report Booklet has instructions for requesting the final examination.

Author of This Course

Rick C. Howard is the pastor of Peninsula Christian Center in Redwood City, California and is also an instructor at Bethany Bible College in Santa Cruz, California. He was ordained by the Assemblies of God in 1961. He has also served on the faculty of Northeastern University, Boston, Massachusetts and Evangel College in Springfield, Missouri. He also served as National College Youth Representative for the General Council of the Assemblies of God, Springfield, Missouri.

In this course he writes from much experience as an author, editor, and Bible instructor. He has traveled extensively throughout the world as a teacher and preacher.

In addition to his teaching and preaching experience, Mr. Howard has authored several books, such as: *The Servant and His Lord, The Koinonia Principle, The 'Christ Cell,* and *Christian Center Principles.*

Mr. Howard earned his A.B. degree at Grove City College in Pennsylvania and his M.A. degree in history at Memphis State University, Memphis, Tennessee.

Your ICI Instructor

Your ICI instructor will be happy to help you in any way possible. If you have any questions about the course or the unit student reports, please feel free to ask him. If several people want to study the course together, ask him about special arrangements for group study.

God bless you as you begin to study *Christian Maturity*. May it enrich your life and Christian service and help you fulfill more effectively your part in the body of Christ.

Unit 1
Pictures of
Christian
Maturity

Godly Desires for Growth

Most fathers and mothers watch eagerly as their children grow. They point with pride to each new sign of growth. Children also long for the day when they will be grown up. Then they are mature enough to accept full rights and duties in the family. From the points of view of both parents and children, nothing is more sad than a lack of normal growth.

All of this is true when applied to our spiritual life as well. God desires a growing fellowship with man. Man also desires this relationship and feels lost without it. Even when he does not understand what he needs, he is searching for this fellowship with God. But he cannot find it until he accepts Jesus Christ as Savior. Then, as a believer he cannot experience the level of fellowship which God desires until he accepts God's purpose for him. That purpose is to be conformed to the image of Jesus Christ. We can say, therefore, that Christian maturity fulfills the desires of both God and man.

Growing up is fun but difficult. I'm sure you remember exciting and happy things about becoming an adult. You haven't forgotten the hard things either, have you? This course, as the Holy Spirit uses it to teach you, will help you grow. You can expect it to challenge you. And as you grow, you will become aware of new rights and more important duties in God's family. Both you and I desire this to happen to us. Let this Scripture be our theme: "When I was a child, my speech, feelings, and thinking were all those of a child; now that I am a man, I have no more use for childish ways" (1 Corinthians 13:11).

lesson outline

God's Desire for Man to Grow
    In Creation
    From the Fall to Redemption
    From the Fall to Maturity
Man's Desire to Grow
Direction of Man's Desire to Grow
    Direction Through Jesus' Life
    Direction Through Assurance of Salvation
    Direction Through Understanding Natural Growth

lesson objectives

When you finish this lesson you should be able to:

- Maintain a fellowship with God which will cause you to grow in Christlikeness.
- Understand better and perform more effectively your own part in your spiritual growth.
- Relate both natural process and supernatural power to Christian maturity.
- Define Christian Maturity.

learning activities

1. Ask the Holy Spirit to guide your study. Remember that He desires to guide you into all truth. (See John 16:13).

2. Before starting this lesson, get a notebook. In it, write the answers to exercises that are too long to include in this independent study textbook, and any other notes you desire to make as you study this course.

3. Read carefully the introductory material in this independent study textbook.

4. Read the inspirational section, outline, objectives, and learning activities of Lesson 1.

5. Look up in the glossary at the end of the textbook the definitions to any key words that you do not understand.

6. Carefully read the lesson development, answering each question as you come to it. After answering each one check your answer with the answer given at the end of the lesson, then correct your answer if necessary.

7. Look up each Scripture reference in the lesson development as soon as you come to it.

8. Take the self-test at the end of the lesson. Check your answers carefully. Review any items answered incorrectly.

key words

Understanding the key words we have listed at the beginning of each lesson will help you as you study. You will find them defined in alphabetical order in the glossary that starts on page 188 in this independent study textbook. If you are in doubt as to the meaning of any of the words on the list, you may look them up now or when you come across them in your reading.

destiny	maturity
dynamic	perfect
evaluation	purpose
fellowship	relationship
grow up	stature
growth	

lesson development

GOD'S DESIRE FOR MAN TO GROW

We will begin our course in Christian maturity by considering God's reason for creating man. Have you ever asked, "Why did God make man in the first place?" Maybe you have wondered, "Just what does God expect from man?"

In Creation

Objective 1. *Explain to someone else why God created man.*

Several times God stopped the process of creating the world to view His own work. Each time He saw that it was good. On the sixth day, God created man according to His plan. Man was made in the image or likeness of God (Genesis 1:27). Then, God could look at His work again and see that it was very good (Genesis 1:31). Without man the creation had been incomplete. The creation of man fulfilled the plan of God. Through fellowship between God and man, a basic need was met for each of them. By means of this fellowship, man would grow in God, glorifying Him, and fulfilling the purpose of his creation.

1 Look up Ecclesiastes 12:13. According to this verse what two things must man do to fulfill God's reason for creating him?

....

....

To "fear God" means to respect and reverence Him. Certainly that includes respect for His purpose for man.

From the Fall to Redemption

Objective 2. *State the goal that God has planned for man to attain through redemption and growth in Jesus Christ.*

Unfortunately the story of creation does not end with man's fulfillment of God's glorious purpose for him. Because of man's sin, he fell and became unable to fellowship with God and glorify Him. The thoughts of fallen man were far from God. His desires led him away from God. His actions were often offensive to God. Sin ruined man by keeping him from the fellowship with God that was God's purpose for him.

But God loved man so much and desired his fellowship so greatly that He provided the plan of salvation. God's plan was to restore the broken fellowship through the sacrifice of His Son, Jesus Christ. God sent His own Son to die for man so that he could be redeemed and again have fellowship with Him.

2 What is the goal for man in God's plan of salvation?

....

The likeness of God in man was damaged by the fall. But through Jesus Christ, God brings man back into His own likeness. This is a major theme of the New Testament. We become like God as we grow into the likeness of Jesus Christ.

From the Fall to Maturity

Objective 3. *Use Ephesians 4:13 to point out the goal of Christian maturity.*

Maturity may be defined as "a state of having been brought by natural processes to completeness of growth and development" or "pertaining to a condition of full development as a man of mature years." As we will see, the natural processes which lead to maturity can be hindered or helped. The ministry of the church of Jesus Christ is to help each believer become a mature person like Jesus Christ. Ephesians 4:11-16, to which we will later devote almost a full chapter, gives this basic truth.

3 According to Ephesians 4:11, who are the ministering persons that Christ has given to help us attain spiritual maturity?

....

....

4 According to Ephesians 4:13, what is the goal of Christian maturity?

....

There are words in this passage listed in the *Key Words*. Make sure you look them up in the glossary.

The word translated "mature" in Ephesians 4:13 is often translated "perfect" (compare Matthew 19:21 and Philippians 3:12 with Colossians 1:28). The word perfect generally means "complete" or "whole." It can also mean "finished" or "accomplished" (see John 19:30).

5 Read Colossians 1:28. Which of the following items best defines the word mature in this verse?
a) Flawless
b) Sinless
c) Whole or complete

The closer we come to being like Christ, the more we fulfill the purpose which God has for our lives, and the more we glorify Him. Can you see why God has such a great desire for each Christian to mature, to become complete and Christlike? Spiritual maturity is the highest goal which God has for each believer's life. Our Heavenly Father eagerly looks for each development toward maturity in our lives.

MAN'S DESIRE TO GROW

Objective 4. *Explain why no man can find complete satisfaction for his need for growth unless he looks to God.*

There is within every man a hunger to find his reason and purpose for being. Much of the restlessness among all people is caused by a search for life's meaning. Man needs a goal. Even when unsaved, a man feels linked with destiny and eternity. He is searching and longing for a satisfaction which can only be fully found in fellowship with God. Human personality can be fully developed only in a God-man relationship that pleases God. As long as man remains apart from God, his desire for spiritual growth cannot be fulfilled.

There is an emptiness inside every unsaved person which is like an alarm or signal placed there by the Creator. When man does not fulfill God's purpose for him, he experiences spiritual distress which may be likened to the physical pain of losing an arm or leg. People often find a temporary escape from such spiritual distress through sin. The temporariness of this escape may be compared to the relief that certain medicines give to physical pain. Man's denial of his need to know and serve the Creator is an act of sin that prevents spiritual maturity.

Our human spirit is in a sense a borrowed godlike nature. Only in our spirit are we truly like God. It is our most precious gift. It is our spirit which demands purpose.

6 The godlikeness or *image of God* in man is man's spirit. (This spirit includes such things as will, mind, choice, etc.) Read 1 Corinthians 2:10-11. What is the part of a person that relates him to God?

....

7 According to Romans 8:16, how does God's Spirit declare to us that we are children of God?

....

We can say that every person is born with a pressing need to be growing toward a goal. Often a person feels this need in terms of schooling, wealth, or status and promotion. In truth this need can be satisfied only by a proper relationship to the Creator. It is met as we become more and more like Him. We are then able to have true fellowship with God. The need or desire in every man for growth is a quality that becomes a godly desire only when man focuses his desire on Christian maturity.

DIRECTION OF MAN'S DESIRE TO GROW

Objective 5. *Tell how a person can use the force of his inborn desire for growth that moves forward in God.*

Have you ever watched someone trying to dam a rapidly flowing river? Sometimes it's almost impossible because there is a great power surging forward which is extremely difficult to stop. That movement is called the dynamic. "Dynamic" is an inner force that demands movement.

God has placed this force within man. Yet, God allows man to choose the direction for this force. You might say that the river of desire within a person moves in various directions seeking its course. People without God are referred to in the Scripture as *forceful moving waters* (Jude 13). Unsaved people use this dynamic for self-goals. These are ultimately unsatisfying. We believers, on the other hand, must learn to use this dynamic to move toward maturity in God.

8 How did the Samaritan in Luke 10:30-35 allow his dynamic of pity to move him forward in God?

....

Direction Through Jesus' Life

Objective 6. *Exercise faith in Christ to fulfill the true purpose of your desire for growth.*

Jesus Christ came into our world as a revelation of God's concern that we find our true purpose. Jesus is a model of the correct "God-man" relationship. His wholeness was the result of a life lived in correct relationship to its source. His life, death, and resurrection opened the way for man to truly *fulfill his purpose.* What sin had robbed from man, Christ restored to him. Through faith in Christ we are born into the family of God and discover the right direction for the *dynamic* of our spirit.

9 In John 10:10 Jesus expressed our true purpose by saying he had come in order that
a)   we might escape hell.
b)   the Scripture might be fulfilled.
c)   we might have life in all its fullness.

Direction Through Assurance of Salvation

Objective 7. *Tell why the basis for your spiritual growth is supernatural.*

Some people think that to be born again is the ultimate Christian goal. But the mere knowledge that we are Christians does not guarantee us a dynamic Christian life! Dynamic living implies being in motion and growing. Just as a newborn baby grows because he has life, so must the new Christian. He now has the possibility to move in the direction God wants him to. But growth is not automatic—the believer must want to grow toward Christian maturity.

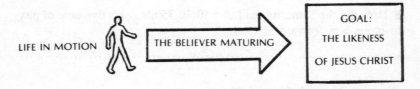

LIFE IN MOTION   THE BELIEVER MATURING   GOAL: THE LIKENESS OF JESUS CHRIST

Your first step toward Christian maturity must be to believe that Jesus' death and resurrection was for the forgiveness of your sins. Your next step is to recognize and confess Jesus Christ as the Lord of your life. The person who believes and confesses receives the Spirit of Christ upon his human spirit as Master and Lord. Then the Holy Spirit gives to him a dynamic drive toward man's true purpose. In this drive man will encounter many obstacles. But through all these obstacles, man can make progress with the Spirit's help toward maturity in Christ.

In 1 Corinthians 3:23, "You belong to Christ" implies that Jesus Christ is your Lord and Master.

10 According to the following texts, why do we belong to Christ?

a 1 Corinthians 6:20 ....

b 1 Peter 1:18-19 ....

c Ephesians 1:4 ....

11 The Bible explains in John 3:19-20 why all the world does not recognize the claims of God through Christ on their lives. Why is this?

....

12 The following three Scriptures tell us what a person must do in order to belong to Christ. By studying these verses you can understand and explain to others how to become a Christian. Read each passage and write down what is necessary to have the new life in Jesus. I have given you the answer to the first one.

a John 3:16-18   *Requires a person to believe in God's only Son.*

b Romans 10:9-10 ....

c John 1:12 ....

The answers to the preceding exercise tell us that *a man can know that he is saved*, that he is born as a child in God's family. Take a moment to read 1 John 4:14-16 to make this truth especially real to you.

13 Now, write in two sentences, using your own words, the truth in 1 John 4:14-16. Write these sentences in your notebook, wording them as if you were explaining this wonderful truth to a friend.

Direction Through Understanding Natural Growth

Objective 8. *Compare spiritual growth with natural growth.*

Christian maturity may be defined as a process, similar to natural growth, whereby we are brought to spiritual completeness.

Our life in Christ is compared to a seed. Growth and maturity are often illustrated by farming and plants in the Bible. When we are born anew, it is through an incorruptible seed. The Bible describes this special seed in 1 Peter 1:23 (King James Version).

14 According to 1 Peter 1:23, through what have we been born again?

....

First John 3:9 (King James Version) refers to God's seed which remains in us as believers. You know that in all life the potential for full growth is in the tiny seed. For example, the potential for the full grown corn plant is in the corn seed. It is hard to believe that a great tree can come from a small seed. Yet it does. The nature of the plant contained in the seed can only be seen through the growth process.

In the newborn believer, potential for his *likeness of God* is the seed of the Word of God. His new life is a dynamic, which can through spiritual growth move onward toward Christian maturity.

15 In 2 Corinthians 9:10, what are the two things that God promises us in the realm of our need for natural sustenance and growth?

....

Remember that just as God can cause the natural seed to grow, so also He can cause spiritual seed within us to grow. And, just as God requires the farmer's labor in the growth of natural seed, so also He requires that the believer's own effort be a part of the process of growth of the spiritual seed within him.

16 Without looking in the text, write out in your notebook your own definition of Christian maturity. Then review the definition of this term at the beginning of this section of the lesson and compare your definition with it.

Notice particularly from the definition of Christian maturity in this text that we are brought to spiritual completeness by a process that is similar to natural processes. The image of God in man—man's spirit—is a dynamic force which was meant to flow within the banks of a proper and wonderful fellowship between creature and Creator.

Although broken by sin, that purpose can now be restored through Jesus Christ.

The Bible tells us clearly that there is a measuring rod for our maturity as Christians.

17 According to Ephesians 4:13, what is the measuring rod for Christian maturity? Circle the letter in front of your answer.
a) Ability to quote Scriptures
b) Living without mistakes
c) Christ's full stature
d) Educational advancement

Perhaps you are asking yourself, "Why isn't Christian growth an easier process?" Again, the answer can be seen in nature. Seed has many natural enemies. It can be buried too deeply or not deeply enough in the soil. Wind can blow it away. The soil can be stony or filled with thistle seed. Many farmers face what seems an impossible task to produce a harvest. The fact remains that good seed will always produce if it is given right conditions.

The greatest enemy of the seed of godlikeness in man is Satan. He is the enemy of any likeness or reflection of God in the world. He designed the temptation which caused man to fall from his original purpose. He directs a world strategy which attempts to keep unsaved men from the gospel. He plans further to keep the Christian from growing in the likeness of Jesus Christ—the goal of Christian maturity.

18 Jesus told a story in Luke 8:4-15 which relates to seed and growth. Please see how many things you can find in this passage which prevented seed from growing.

....

....

Do you think that any of the things mentioned in our answer to the preceding question are symbols of things or situations that are keeping you from spiritual growth?

19 God has provided us with a number of resources that will help make our lives dynamic. These resources may be described as gifts, talents, opportunities, etc. Please evaluate yourself as to how well you are using the following resources to help you grow spiritually (see illustration):

RESOURCE	MUCH	SOME	NONE
STUDY OF GOD'S WORD			
PRAYER			
ATTENDING WORSHIP SERVICES			
FELLOWSHIP WITH OTHER BELIEVERS			
YOUR INBORN DESIRE FOR GROWTH			
YOUR OBEDIENCE TO GOD			

Don't read further until you have completed the above personal evaluation exercise. Now, *pray that the Holy Spirit will help you to mature through diligent use of these resources for spiritual growth.*

To truly glorify the Father in our spiritual life, we must accept the goal of true Christian maturity in our lives. We must decide to reach this goal with the strength and determination of a team attempting to score against their opponent. We can't accept second best.

20 An important verse for us is 2 Peter 3:18. Read this Scripture then fill in the missing words. But continue to .... in the

.... and .... of our Lord and Savior Jesus Christ. To him be the .... now and forever! Amen.

Let us desire the full Christian maturity which can be ours through the grace of God. *And may this Christian service course enable us to help others grow in the likeness of Christ.*

self-test

After you have reviewed this lesson, take the self-test. Then check your answers with those given in the back of the textbook. Review any questions answered incorrectly.

TRUE-FALSE. Write **T** in the blank space before each true statement. Write **F** if the statement is false.

... **1** Creation was complete even without the creation of man.

... **2** Man can never be restored to Godlikeness.

... **3** Man's purpose cannot be truly fulfilled without a proper relationship with God.

... **4** The Christian experience is a guarantee that life will be dynamic.

... **5** A requirement for being born again is to confess Jesus Christ as Lord in a person's life.

MULTIPLE CHOICE. Circle the letter of the correct answer or answers.

6 Indicate the proper understanding of the word *perfect* or *mature* in the Scriptures. (More than one may be correct.)
a) Full grown
b) Sinless
c) Complete
d) Whole
e) Finished
f) Childish

7 The area of man's nature which demands a purpose or reason for being is his
a) soul
b) body.
c) spirit.

8 The purpose of Jesus Christ's coming into our world can best be stated by which two of the following expressions?
a) That man might be condemned
b) As a model of a correct God-man relationship
c) That man might be brought into abundant life
d) To form an important new religion

SHORT ANSWER. Fill in the blank, providing the proper answer to each question.

9 The greatest enemy of the seed of godlikeness in man is:

....

....

10 Name at least two of the types of soil that Jesus described in Luke 8 which represent how men receive the gospel.

....

....

for your notes

answers to the study questions

1 Fear God and obey His commandments.

11 Because men in darkness reject the light.

2 To restore fellowship between God and man.

12 a See example.
   b Confess Jesus as Lord and believe in His resurrection.
   c Receive Christ and believe in Him.

3 Apostles, prophets, evangelists, pastors, and teachers.

13 The truth in 1 John 4:14-16 in your own words.

4 Christlikeness.

14 The living and eternal Word of God.

5 c) Whole or complete.

15 Plenty of seed and a rich harvest.

6 That person's own spirit.

16 A definition of Christian maturity in your own words.

7 By joining Himself to our spirit.

17 c) Christ's full stature.

8 By using his pity in an unselfish manner to help someone in need.

18 The seed fell along the path, was stepped on, was eaten by birds, fell on rocky ground with no moisture, and among choking thorns.

9 c) we might have life in all its fullness.

19 Your own evaluation of yourself.

10 a Because Christ bought us for a price.
   b Because the price Christ paid for us was the costly sacrifice of His own life.
   c Because God chose us to be His through Christ.

20 grow, grace, knowledge, glory.

Lesson 2

Jesus Christ: An Illustration of Growth

Do you remember a time when you really pleased a parent or a teacher with some evidence of growth? Have you ever seen a little boy trying to stand tall beside his father? I remember visiting one home where the two boys had marked the father's height on the wall. Below it were a variety of dates and measurements to compare the boys' progress. We have seen that our Heavenly Father desires our maturity so that we may fellowship with Him. We need to grow and fulfill the purpose for which God created us in His image.

But perhaps *maturing as a believer* seems hard to understand. "What does Christian maturity look like?" you may ask. The little boys I just mentioned had a visual goal. They knew their father. They could measure his height. It was not hard for them to picture their own progress toward his likeness.

That's our purpose in this lesson. We want to clearly define Christian maturity in terms of goals which we can visualize. The Bible is an open book. Jesus often taught in parables which were word-pictures taken from the people's common experiences. We will discover that the Bible's standards for growth are clear and relate to each one of us.

lesson outline

Getting a Goal to Grow Toward
Seeing How Jesus Grew
    Physical Maturity
    Mental Maturity
    Social Maturity
    Spiritual Maturity
Learning About Jesus' Image

lesson objectives

When you finish this lesson you should be able to:

■ Identify four ways in which Jesus Christ is a realistic goal for our spiritual growth.

■ State a very practical way in which every Christian can be like Jesus.

■ Experience personal growth toward the likeness of Jesus.

learning activities

1. Read the lesson in this textbook.

2. Look up in the glossary the definitions to any key words that you do not understand.

3. Do the exercises in the lesson development, referring as needed to the textbook. Check your answers periodically with those given in the textbook.

4. Take your Christian Maturity notebook and divide two pages (one across from the other) into four columns. Head each column with one of the following words: 1) *physical*, 2) *mental*, 3) *social*, and 4) *spiritual*. When directed in the lesson development, write out passages of Scripture in these columns.

5. Take the self-test at the end of this lesson, and check your answers carefully. Review those items answered incorrectly.

key words

While reading the Bible or other books, have you encountered words you didn't understand? Do you make it a practice to look up such words in the dictionary? You will have a better understanding of this course if you continually use your dictionary and the glossary of key words at the end of this independent study textbook. You might want to write new words and their definitions in your personal notebook as an added help in remembering them.

adulterous
homosexual
image

lesson development

GETTING A GOAL TO GROW TOWARD

Objective 1: *State the Bible goal for which every Christian must work.*

We have already seen in Ephesians 4:13 that God intends us to "become mature people, reaching to the very height of Christ's full stature." The original language of the New Testament is actually "a mature manhood" or we might say a complete person or a fully grown person.

1 According to this verse what is the actual measurement of that maturity? (Circle the correct answer.)

a) A special spiritual gift

b) The mature manhood of Christ

c) Sinless perfection

The word *stature* is an important one. It means "height or quality gained by growth." Jesus Christ was not born among us as a perfected human being, but as a baby who had to grow like each of us.

2 Hebrews 5:8 refers to Jesus. It begins with these words, "But even though he was God's Son." Write the rest of this verse here.

. . . .

. . . .

3 Review the meaning in the glossary of the word *perfect*. The word perfect means "to complete" or "to bring to final form." How do you think this word may be applied to Jesus?

. . . .

. . . .

Since Jesus always had sinless spiritual perfection He is a perfect model for our own growth in all areas of life (2 Corinthians 5:21). Although we cannot expect to reach sinless spiritual perfection, Christlikeness is a realistic goal for our spiritual growth because working toward a goal that is higher than we can expect to reach will help us to accomplish more than would a lower goal.

4 Read carefully Hebrews 4:14-16. Is Jesus able to identify with the problems of our growing up as Christians? Explain.

. . . .

. . . .

You can see why Jesus is often referred to as our brother (Hebrews 2:11-12,17). If you have an older brother, you know how important an influence he can have as the first born and thus first "maturing" one in the family.

Carefully read Hebrews 2:10 and write it in your notebook. Do you see that Jesus, having grown or been made perfect, is thereby able to lead other sons into God's full purpose? Doesn't that encourage you in your own desire to grow up as a Christian?

SEEING HOW JESUS GREW

Objective 2: *List four specific ways in which Jesus grew.*

We have seen that Jesus Christ is to be our example, and His stature our goal. To be specific, the Bible shows that Jesus grew or matured in four basic areas.

5 Read Luke 2:52. List the four areas in which Jesus grew.

. . . .

. . . .

Can you relate these four areas to areas in which you must grow? Do you see why the verse we learned in 2 Peter 3:18 tells us to grow in the "knowledge of our Lord and Savior Jesus Christ"? As we learn about His life we will better understand the goal and purpose of our own maturity as believers.

Now, you are to begin to fill in the two pages in your notebook as assigned in item number 4 of the learning activities. As you study the next three sections, write out in each of the first three columns on these pages the passages of Scripture as directed.

Physical Maturity

Objective 3: *Form habits that will help you to attain Christian physical maturity.*

The Bible teaches us that Christian maturity in the physical sense involves much more than the simple growth of the body. It involves an understanding of the purpose of the body. Physical maturity for the believer involves the conduct of the body in a way pleasing to God the Father. The following Scriptures will help you to understand this area and form Christian physical habits: 1 Thessalonians 4:3-8; 1 Corinthians 6:9-15, 18-19; 1 Timothy 4:8; Galatians 6:7-8. *Please write these Scriptures in your notebook under the heading "Physical."*

6 What does 1 Corinthians 6:9-10 say about the destiny of those who abuse their bodies in immorality?
a) They will be severely punished.
b) They are to be excluded from the church.
c) They shall not possess God's kingdom.

Mental Maturity

Objective 4: *Develop Christian mental maturity by filling your mind with good thoughts.*

The human mind is a wonderful gift from God. Yet, have you ever noticed how difficult it is to keep the mind under control. It is so easy to allow the mind to wander and even to think unchristian thoughts. No wonder that Peter told the Christians "Have your minds ready for action. Keep alert" (1 Peter 1:13). You see, Jesus teaches us that the mind is really a problem area in our lives.

7 Read Mark 7:18-23. According to Jesus where do all sorts of evil things that a person does come from?

. . . .
. . . .

In fact, letting our minds dwell on evil things can be sinful.

Write out Matthew 5:28, 1 Peter 1:13, Mark 7:18-23, Proverbs 23:7, and 2 Corinthians 10:4-5, in your notebook column titled *"Mental."*

8 In 2 Corinthians 10:4-5 Paul tells how "to destroy strongholds," then lists three ways to develop Christian mental maturity. What are they?

a . . . .

b ....

c .... :

9 In Philippians 4:8, how many kinds of things are mentioned that we should fill our minds with?
a) Three
b) Eight
c) Twelve

Now carefully read Romans 12:1-2. Notice the last phrase " . . . know the will of God—what is good and is pleasing to Him and is perfect." Here is that word *perfect* again which, you remember, means "mature" or "complete and whole." We must try through our own will to know God's will, to know how He wants us to live.

10 According to Romans 12:2, how does God transform the person who has been living by the standards of this world?

....

You can see how important it is to be mature in our mind.

Social Maturity

Objective 5: *Make progress toward Christian social maturity.*

Christian growth involves the social aspect of our lives as well as the physical and mental aspects. You could list many areas of your social experience: family, friends, marriage, relations to government, neighbors, and so forth. It would be impossible to list or discuss in this course all the Scriptures in this area.

Write out in your notebook column titled *"Social,"* Psalm 101, James 4:4-5, and Ephesians chapter 5. (Yes, the entire chapter!)

NOTE: This great chapter (Ephesians 5) begins by exhorting us to try to conduct ourselves without fault (verse 1) then mentions evil things we must not do (verses 3-5). Verse 11 emphasizes how we should react to worthless things that people do: "Have nothing to do with . . . things that belong to the darkness." The chapter closes with instructions on godliness in the marriage relationship (verses 21-33).

11 Read Psalm 101 aloud. Now, prayerfully choose one area of the Psalmist's life in this psalm which you would like to strengthen in your life. (Examples: honesty, dealings with evil, purity of life in the family, etc.)

. . . .

God is concerned to help you grow in each area of your life.

Spiritual Maturity

Objective 6: *Choose habits, thoughts, and relationships that will help you on your way toward spiritual maturity.*

This entire course is on this subject! Lesson 6 will discuss spiritual maturity in detail. We will not define it here. But please remember when you study Lesson 6 to write Scripture passages in your notebook column titled *"Spiritual."*

This illustration sums up what we have studied:

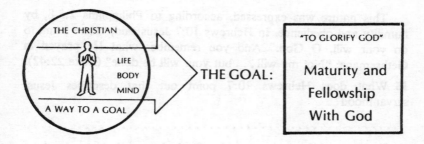

Look at the Illustration and you will see that the Christian's goal is outside himself. To reach the Christian goal, we must move toward that goal.

12 Does the illustration above describe a dynamic life? (Explain)

. . . .

Every decision I make concerning habits, thoughts, and relationships must be made in view of *The Goal of Spiritual Maturity.*

LEARNING ABOUT JESUS' IMAGE

Objective 7: *Describe the servanthood of Jesus and identify yourself as His servant.*

Some biblical principles seem hard to understand. We have already discovered that God has set us apart "to become many brothers" (Romans 8:29). Perhaps you are asking, "How can I be like Jesus?" That question arises when we remember that He was sinless and God in human form. Let us understand a simple but important point: It is in the role of servants that we become like Jesus.

13 Read Philippians 2:5-8. According to Philippians 2:5, what attitude or mind are we to have?

. . . .

14 According to Philippians 2:6-8, what nature did Jesus willingly take on?

. . . .

This nature was expressed, according to Philippians 2:5-8, by humility and obedience. In Hebrews 10:7 Jesus said, "Here I am, to do your will, O God." And you remember what He prayed in Gethsemane: "Not my will . . . but your will be done" (Luke 22:42).

15 What does Hebrews 10:7 point out that describes Jesus' servanthood?

. . . .

Do you understand now why Paul, James, Jude, and others identified themselves as "servants of Jesus Christ"? That is how we become like Jesus. We are not saved from sin for the sake of our own salvation only, we are saved to serve. We accept a relationship of obedience to one Lord, Jesus Christ. He, indeed, becomes our *Master* and we become love-servants to His will. Salvation with its joys, victory, and freedom is more than an experience. Through salvation we are brought into the true understanding of our purpose. We are created to glorify God. Our goal is to be conformed to Jesus Christ and thus restored to true fellowship with God. Such a relationship fulfills man's deepest desire for purpose in life. We should all declare with Paul the apostle: "With my whole being I shall bring honor to Christ, whether I live or die" (Philippians 1:20).

self-test

TRUE-FALSE. Write **T** in the blank·space if the statement is true. Write **F** if it is false. Then, change the FALSE statements to make them true.

... 1 Stature is a word that means "height or quality gained by growth."

Stature is a word that means ....

... 2 According to Jesus all sorts of evil things come from within a person's heart.

According to Jesus all sorts of evil things come from

....

... 3 The Bible teaches us that the Christian believer is to have the mind or attitude of Moses.

The Bible teaches us that the believer is to have the mind or attitude of ....

MULTIPLE CHOICE. Circle the letter(s) before the correct choice(s) to each question.

4 The Bible teaches in Luke 2:52 that Jesus grew in four areas of His life. Select these four areas from the words below.
a) Spiritual
b) Physical
c) Emotional
d) Mental
e) Medical
f) Biblical
g) Psychological
h) Social

5 According to 1 Corinthians 6:9-10, certain uses of our body will keep us from possessing God's kingdom. Select those uses from this series of descriptive words.
a) Immoral
b) Athletic
c) Tiring
d) Adulterous
e) Homosexual
f) Thinking

6 Philippians 2:5-8 indicates that Jesus Christ willingly took upon Himself not only a human form but also a very special nature. What was it?
a) That of a priest
b) That of a servant
c) That of a king
d) That of a prophet

SHORT ANSWER. Write in the proper answer to the question on the lines provided.

7 The believer should relate under the Lordship of Jesus Christ to what four classifications of persons in his social experiences?

a ....

b ....

c ....

d ....

answers to the study questions

1 b) The mature manhood of Christ.

9 b) Eight.

2 "he learned through his sufferings to be obedient."

10 By a complete change of his mind.

3 To the full development of His physical and mental characteristics and work.

11 Your own answer.

4 Yes, because He was tempted as we are and can feel sympathy for our weakness.

12 Yes, because both dynamic life and Illustration 2.1 indicate a life that moves toward a goal.

5 In body, in wisdom, in favor with God, and in favor with man.

13 The attitude of Jesus Christ.

6 c) They shall not possess God's kingdom.

14 The nature of a servant.

7 From within his heart where evil ideas and thoughts have their source.

15 His obedience.

8 **a** Destroy false arguments.
   b Pull down obstacles to the knowledge of God.
   c Make every thought obey Christ.

for your notes

Lesson 3

Further Illustrations
of Growth

The primary illustration of Christian maturity in the Bible is Jesus Christ. He is our elder brother. He took the form of a servant, and obeyed the Father perfectly. He humbled Himself with the death of the cross. We Christians are to be conformed to the likeness of Jesus Christ. This is the eventual goal of Christian maturity. The believer lives his life to do the will of Jesus Christ. This is revealed by the Word of God and the Holy Spirit. The "likeness of Jesus Christ" applies to the physical, mental, and social parts of our lives as well as to the spiritual part.

But the Bible illustrates our Christian growth in other ways too. In this lesson we will study several other illustrations. These will include the family, farming, and building. Our purpose is to see the concept of Christian maturity as clearly as possible.

Perhaps you have seen a great hill or mountain. From a distance it looks rather close. You think you can be there in a short time. As you approach it the distance seems much greater. We sometimes call this perspective or point-of-view. We are trying to see our subject from several perspectives—several approaches. Allow the Holy Spirit to make the right one for you especially real.

lesson outline

We Grow Up in a Family
    Starting As a Baby
    Changing Our Diet
    Accepting Different Roles
We Are Like a Valuable Farm
    Belonging to God
    Carrying Out Responsibility
We Are a Building of God
    Foundation and Building
    How to Build God's Building

lesson objectives

When you finish this lesson you should be able to:

■ Recognize the main source of the believer's spiritual growth.

■ Understand the importance of the believer's cooperation with God in the process of spiritual growth.

learning activities

1. Check the glossary at the end of your study textbook for definitions to any key words that you do not understand.

2. If a concept in this lesson seems difficult, read the section twice or more. Use your pencil to underline or mark important parts of the lesson development.

3. Work carefully through the study questions, writing your own answers in pencil *before* checking the correct responses.

4. Ask the Holy Spirit to make these examples of growing-up very real to you.

5. Take the self-test at the end of this lesson, and check your answers carefully.

key words

architect	conviction
artisan	cultivate
"brokenness"	repentance
childish	responsibility
conformed	viewpoint

lesson development

WE GROW UP IN A FAMILY

Every human life has parents. There must be a father and mother who have given life to it, and who have the responsibility of caring for it. The human infant is born with a great deal of need for care.

Starting As a Baby

Objective 1: *State how a new Christian can grow from a spiritual baby toward Christian maturity.*

Have you noticed an infant recently? Think of the various things which must be done for the child to keep it alive and healthy. Parents gladly provide for the infant, knowing that it will eventually mature. A new Christian has been "born again" (John 3:3). Scripture refers to him as a *baby*. He must partake of spiritual food in order to grow from spiritual infancy into spiritual maturity.

1 Read John 3:3-6. What is the source of our spiritual birth?

....

Notice in John 3:6 that John contrasts physical birth "of human parents" with spiritual birth.

When you thought about an infant a moment ago, you may have remembered hearing its screams when hungry. God's Word describes this reaction in the new Christian.

2 Take a moment to study 1 Peter 2:2. Please note that the phrase "grow up and be saved" is better understood as translated in the New International Version: "Grow up in your salvation." According to this verse, what can we expect of a truly born again person?

....

Changing Our Diet

Objective 2: *Explain how a Christian can gain understanding of more advanced spiritual truth.*

It is clear in the Scripture that the believer is neither to remain a spiritual baby, nor to continue to use spiritual milk. Let us examine several Scriptures which we shall develop more completely later.

3 Look first at 1 Corinthians 3:1-3. Please circle the letter before the correct answer. This passage indicates
a) that mature Christians no longer need spiritual milk.
b) that mature Christians continue to need spiritual milk.
c) nothing definite concerning mature Christians and spiritual milk.

4 Now read aloud an important message in Hebrews 5:11-14. Here again the Christians are still using "milk" and not "solid food." Verse 13 indicates that a milk-drinking Christian is
a) experienced in the matter of right.
b) still a child.
c) experienced in the matter of wrong.

5 What does Hebrews 5:14 imply that mature Christians can do which milk-drinking Christians cannot do?

. . . .

Perhaps you are asking, "But what is the difference between spiritual milk and spiritual solid-food?"Ask yourself where milk comes from. You will answer that it comes from a body which has eaten solid food and produces milk. Milk has gone through the digestive system of another: the mother, for example. Milk to a Christian is primary spiritual truth as opposed to more advanced spiritual truth. Understanding of more advanced truth comes through practical application of already known primary truth (see 1 John 1:6-7).

6 Turn to 1 Corinthians 14:20. The apostle commends a childlike attitude toward evil. But he urges the believers to not be like . . . . in their . . . .

7 Again in 1 Corinthians 13:11 we are urged to grow up. In what three ways does a child reveal himself according to this verse?

. . . .

Paul continues in this verse by saying, "Now that I am a man, I have no more use for childish ways." Do you remember when you put away play things or clothes you used as a child? It was not always easy. Growing up *can be painful.*

Accepting Different Roles

Objective 3: *List three things included in the process of our growing up spiritually.*

God's concern for the believer to achieve full spiritual stature is found in many places in the Bible. God is concerned that the believer knows the full purpose He has for His children. The apostles shared God's yearning father-heart. Paul and John particularly sought to move the believer through childhood into young manhood and on to fatherhood.

Do you remember the changes of duties in your family as you became older? Are you now a mother or father yourself? If so, your view of life certainly differs from that of a child or youth. The apostle John writes from the position of a spiritual father in 1 John 2:12-13.

8 Read 1 John 2:12-13 carefully. Select the three stages John refers to from the following list. Circle the letter before each one of the correct three.
a) Babies
b) Children
c) Old men
d) Young men
e) Boys
f) Fathers

You can see in 1 John 2:12-13 that the situations are different at each of the three levels of maturity. The children *receive* forgiveness for their sins; the young men *do* a notable deed in their victory over evil, and the fathers *know* God better than the others. The children are portrayed as the *most dependent*, the young men as the *most active*, and the fathers as the *most mature*. Fathers have fullest understanding of God and His purposes.

You have noticed that three levels of growth in God's family are represented in this passage. And three things included in the process of our growing up spiritually are *reaching higher levels of knowledge, accepting more responsibility,* and *performing more significant duties.* As we have seen, *growing* means "leaving," leaving childish things to gain greater stature.

CHILDREN-RECEIVE   YOUNG MEN-DO   FATHERS-KNOW

WE ARE LIKE A VALUABLE FARM

You know that some farm land is much more valuable than other land. Good land with rich soil and well-watered plains is very precious. The farmer's very life is built around his land. He clears and plows, plants and cultivates, waters and waits. The harvest is his reward. He has worked hard during long hours. The farmer deserves the joy of a good harvest. How sad it is when his efforts are in vain and the land or climate robs him of his due reward.

Belonging to God

Objective 4: *Explain how Ephesians 3:17-18 indicates that we belong to God.*

The Bible often refers to God's people as being the Lord's vineyard or field (Isaiah 5:1-7; Jeremiah 12:10). God has chosen us and we are His field. He has carefully planted His seed in the soil of our lives. He expects and deserves to have a harvest. He awaits our maturity as anxiously as the farmer observes his crops.

9 Read 1 Corinthians 3:9. According to the first sentence in this verse, believers are God's field. Now read verses 5-8 of the same chapter. Notice the phrases: "sowed the seed," "watered the plant," "grow." According to these verses, who makes the plant grow? Circle the letter of the correct answer.
a) Apollos
b) God
c) Man
d) Partners

NOTE: Don't forget that although God alone has the power to develop spiritual growth in us, He requires our cooperation with Him in developing it.

Ephesians 3:17-18 is a prayer by the apostle Paul that the believers may have their *roots* in love, so that they "together with all God's people, may have the power to understand how broad and lcng, how high and deep, is Christ's love." To have our *roots in God's love* denotes that we belong to God and continues the analogy between believers and a valuable farm. God's love, like rich soil, will help growth. In this passage Paul is praying for what God awaits in us: *Christian maturity.*

Carrying Out Responsibility

Objective 5: *Describe the responsibility to God's field that we must carry out in order to reap God's harvest of blessing.*

The believer is sometimes pictured as the keeper of the field of God. He has a responsibility to carry out as a workman in God's field. You remember reading in 1 Corinthians 3 that Paul sowed seed, Apollos watered, and so forth.

10 In Jeremiah 4:3, what is God telling His people to do that refers in a literal sense to farming?

....

The answer to the preceding question means that we can make the spiritual soil of our life ready to receive God's seed. Perhaps you ask, "How can I plow the soil of my life?" *Plowing breaks up soil to eliminate its hard crust.* Then both seed and moisture can enter into the soil and cause growth. Brokenness in the believer's life is a result of responding in humility to God's conviction. Such response keeps the soil of his heart open. The Holy Spirit will faithfully tell or show (convict) our spirit when something is wrong.

Can you remember a recent time in your life when the Holy Spirit convicted you? Perhaps it was because of something you said. Or maybe you were angry or bitter toward a fellow believer. How did you respond to this? Did you excuse yourself? Did you resist the conviction? An attitude of brokenness in true humility responds with repentance to God's conviction.

Repentance means "to turn away from." An illustration of brokenness and repentance in response to God's conviction is found in the following *prayer*:

Thank you, Holy Spirit, for showing me this sin. I am genuinely sorry for this wrong. I repent and turn from this. Thank you that I am forgiven through the price of Christ Jesus' sacrifice. Praise you, Father.

Through brokenness and repentance the soil of my life is kept open and permits spiritual growth.

11 Read another verse concerning this matter: Hosea 10:12. This is a wonderful command from God to his people. According to this verse, what are the people to plant and reap?

....

Our responsibility to God's field is to plow and plant in devotion to the Lord. When we carry out these responsibilities, we are blessed with God's abundant harvest.

WE ARE A BUILDING OF GOD

Perhaps near where you live, there is a very grand building. Does it stand above all others in size? Is it made of more beautiful materials? No doubt it was built with the skill and care of dedicated workmen. Its perfection shows it was built to an exact design. People like to look at it. Some other buildings are built more quickly, with less skill, and contain less costly materials. They are less durable. Anyone can tell the difference.

12 Quote the part of 1 Corinthians 3:9 that relates most closely to this section of the lesson.

....

Foundation and Building

Objective 6: *Use 1 Corinthians 3:12 to explain to someone else the operation of man's free will in the choice of materials for God's spiritual building.*

In 1 Corinthians 3:9-12, Paul places special emphasis on three things:

1. God's building.
2. Foundation for God's building.
3. Materials in God's building.

Notice the specific difference between the composition of the foundation for this building and the composition of the building upon that foundation.

13 Who is the foundation which is laid for this building (verse 11)?

....

14 What are the six building materials listed in this passage (verse 12)?

a ....

b ....

c ....

d ....

e ....

f ....

We saw above that we are both God's field and the keeper of His field. Now we understand that we are both His building and His builders. It is significant that man can exercise his own free will in the choice of materials he uses in the building of God's building. In one sense the great building we are working on is the church (the body of Jesus Christ in the world—not a physical building). In another sense our own body is like a church.

15 Read 1 Corinthians 6:19-20. What is our body compared to in these verses? Circle the letter of the correct answer.
a) A growing field of grain
b) A tall fruit-bearing tree
c) A pearl of great price
d) The temple of the Holy Spirit

How to Build God's Building

Now, read 1 Corinthians 3:13-17, and answer the following questions.

16 What is it about man's work on God's building that will be judged?
a) The amount
b) The quality
c) The beauty

17 The illustration of God's judgment upon our work says that in the Day of Christ every man's work will be exposed and revealed by .... We are further told that "if what was built on the foundation survives the fire, the builder will receive a ...."

Every day, I must choose how and what to build. The foundation cannot be changed. It is Jesus Christ our Lord. The Father has a wonderful plan for what my personal *Christian building* should be like. He tells me in His Word of the right attitudes, habits, words, and character. He designed what a Christian should be like. When I build to His specifications (the specific orders on *His* plan), the *building* of my life will be beautiful and durable. It will be like the grand building we talked about. If I neglect God's plan and choose materials that do not please Him (wood, grass, or straw), my building will not survive fire and I will never become a mature Christian.

Perhaps you would like to pray this prayer with me:

Father, your plan is best. The materials you choose are best. I want the building of my life to be made to your standard. I want to be conformed to your Son Jesus Christ in my body, mind, and spirit. Amen.

self-test

SHORT ANSWER. Write in the proper answer to the question on the lines provided.

1 At what point in his experience should a believer no longer need the *milk* of the Word of God?

2 MATCHING. Match the Scripture to each of the basic ideas brought out in this lesson by writing the correct number in each blank space. (I have filled in the first blank for you.)

1) "Anyone who has to drink milk is still a child, without experience in the matter of right and wrong."

2) "I am writing to you, fathers, because you know him who has existed from the beginning."

3) "Plough up your unploughed fields; do not sow your seeds among thorns."

4) "Each one must be careful how he builds . . . Some will use gold or silver or precious stones in building."

. .2. **a** A fuller level of maturity is to have a fuller knowledge of God and His purpose.

. . . **b** Believers choose the material which they use to build their life upon the foundation of Christ.

. . . **c** The soil of our life can be kept open by responding in humility to the conviction of God.

. . . **d** An understanding of more advanced spiritual truth must be added to our knowledge of primary truth in order to understand more difficult problems.

MULTIPLE CHOICE. Select the correct letters before the correct choices to each question.

3 In this lesson, the believer is compared to several things by way of illustration. Select the five correct illustrations.

a) A tree

b) A baby

c) God's field

d) A ship

e) An island

f) Soil

g) An old man

h) God's building

i) A road

j) The temple of the Holy Spirit

4 Select the three building materials which represent those qualities which will LAST at the Judgment Seat of Christ.

a) Gold

b) Grass

c) Straw

d) Wood

e) Silver

f) Precious Stones

answers to the study questions

1 The Spirit of God.

10 To plow up their unplowed fields.

2 Thirst for pure spiritual milk.

11 They are to plant righteousness and reap blessings.

3 a) that mature Christians no longer need spiritual milk.

12 "You are ... God's building."

4 b) still a child.

13 Jesus Christ.

5 Distinguish between good and evil.

14 a) Gold.
   b) Silver.
   c) Precious stones.
   d) Wood.
   e) Grass.
   f) Straw.

6 children, thinking.

15 d) The temple of the Holy Spirit.

7 In speech, feelings, and thinking.

16 b) The quality.

8 b) Children.
   d) Young men.
   f) Fathers.

17 fire, reward.

9 b) God.

for your notes

FURTHER ILLUSTRATIONS OF GROWTH

for your notes

Lesson 4

Hindrance and Help to Christian Growth

After the last lesson you should feel somewhat like a son growing up, a valuable piece of land being carefully farmed, or a great and beautiful building under construction. Which likeness do you most identify with? No matter! In a sense, we are like all three at once! Each illustration describes exciting potentials for Christian growth.

One part of this lesson is meant to show you from Scripture things that cause Christian maturity to be delayed or even stopped entirely. Recognizing these causes will help us identify them in our own life. Knowing why we are not growing spiritually can help us use our will to bring about change.

Another part of this lesson is a list of things which aid spiritual growth. Knowing these things we can then cooperate with the Holy Spirit to cause our new life in Christ to grow. Together we should find encouragement and help in this study.

lesson outline

That Which Hinders Our Growth
  Wrong Timing
  Wrong Exercise of Will
  Lack in Diet
That Which Helps Our Growth
  The Holy Spirit Our Helper
  The Holy Spirit Working Through Our Spirit

lesson objectives

When you finish this lesson you should be able to:

- Recognize ways in which Christian growth can be hindered.
- Understand more fully the Holy Spirit's part in a Christian's growth.
- Describe the relationship between the Holy Spirit and your spirit that will develop the fruit of the Spirit in you.

learning activities

1. Read the lesson in this independent-study textbook.

2. Do the exercises in the lesson development. Check your answers periodically with those given in this textbook.

3. Take the self-test at the end of this lesson and check your answers carefully. Review those items answered incorrectly.

key words

automatic   negligence
hinder   rational
hindrance   sift

lesson development

THAT WHICH HINDERS OUR GROWTH

There are enemies of natural growth; we have briefly studied this in reference to soil and building. The Bible is direct about some areas which hinder Christian maturity. We need to know them. Perhaps you remember when you were a child and your parents had to teach you about harmful things. Maybe they were telling you to avoid certain plants or animals. The first thing they had to do was to teach you to recognize them. Let us identify some things that hinder spiritual growth.

Wrong Timing

Objective 1: *State what caused the people's retarded spiritual condition in Hebrews 5:12.*

The new birth begins a time of spiritual childhood. Have you ever seen children "dressing up" in adult clothes or pretending to be grown-up? It's humorous to see them walking about in too large shoes or sandals, or pulling a hat over their ears. Sometimes we say to such children, "Wait until you're older to do these things." *Timing* is important. We must not only be concerned with doing right  things but also with doing them *when the time is right*. And wrong timing refers not only to premature action but also to retarded condition. Hebrews 5:12 presents an outstanding example of retarded spiritual condition because of lack of application of present knowledge of God toward further spiritual progress.

1 After reading Hebrews 5:11-14 underline verse 12. What was the people's problem as described in this verse?

....

There are two types of time. The Greeks, in whose language the New Testament was written, thought of time in two basic ways: (1) *chronos* signified a succession of minutes, hours, and days; and (2) *kairos* referred to crisis periods. These periods included such important times as growing, testing, and other experiences in a man's life.

CHRONOS — TIME   KAIROS — CRISIS

In the process of Christian maturity, both of these ideas of time are important. God expects certain things of us based on the actual length of time we have been a Christian. He is in charge of our times of crisis also. Read Ecclesiastes 3:1-8 concerning God's control of times and seasons.

How long has it been since you were born again? Perhaps it was very recently. Or, I wonder if perhaps you have been a Christian a long time. Just remember that the *actual time is important*. We should not expect more of ourselves than God does. Growing up is a time-consuming process. Lack of enough time can be a limiting factor in growing up. But if you have not shown enough progress, don't despair. Ask the Lord to help you through this course to faithfully apply your present knowledge of spiritual things toward further maturity in Christ.

Often the Bible speaks of time as being fulfilled or mature. Ephesians 1:10 is an example: "This plan, which God will complete when the time is right, is to bring all creation together, everything in heaven and on earth, with Christ as head."

2 Who must complete the plan mentioned in Ephesians 1:10?

....

How encouraging to believe that God controls all aspects of the believer's time!

Kairos, periods of crisis, come at irregular times that only God can order. They bring circumstances that teach us.

3 Read Luke 22:31. Here is a very important idea. The subject is *testing*. Who asked permission to test the disciples?
a) Satan
b) God
c) Fellow believers

Who gave permission to test Jesus' disciples? (This question is not directly answered in Luke 22:31, but you need to think about it.) God gave permission to Satan to test the disciples just as He had given him permission to test Job (Job 1:6-12).

The object of this test in Luke 22:31 was to sift the disciples, and Peter in particular. In the following verse we see that Jesus was praying for Peter, in his moment of *kairos*, that he would come through it. Not just to survive, but to be stronger and strengthen others. Let us pray that we, also, may show the endurance in crisis that produces spiritual growth in us and in others.

4 According to Romans 5:3-4 what is it that produces endurance?

....

5 Complete the following statement on the basis of Romans 5:4.

Learning to endure will bring God's . . . . of our life, and from that will come hope.

God allows and arranges times of pressure and times of crisis which are opportunities for us to grow toward Christian maturity.

Wrong Exercise of Will

Objective 2. *Point out a specific wrong exercise of the human will in its relationship with the will of God.*

Why are you studying this course? If maturity were automatic, why should anyone try to mature? You already know the answer. God arranges the *kairos* (crisis), but we must decide how to respond to it. When God created us, He gave us a will. This is the highest aspect of our spirit. God has chosen not to violate the rights of this quality He has given us.

6 Let us return to Hebrews 5:11-14 for a moment. According to verse 11, why was it hard for the writer to explain spiritual truth to the Hebrews?

....

The verb "are" in the original language of verse 11 is better translated, "have become." The Hebrews were not always dull, slow, and hard to move. The Greek word for slow, *nothros*, means "hard to push." Here is what was being said: *There are many truths that cannot be given because you have become slow and hard to move.*

You can see that these Hebrews had a *choice* in the matter. Their *will* was involved. They had hardened their heart against the process of growing up. Again in the last part of verse 12 is the concept that the people were slow to understand. They had to have milk and could not take solid food. In a way, it seems fair to say that most Christians are as mature as they *will* make up their minds to be. God provides the school, but we decide whether or not to learn!

7 Read again Luke 22:31-32 and complete this sentence: Jesus prayed that Peter's faith would ....

8 Read Jesus' words to His disciples in Luke 21:34-36. Notice how many things the disciples must decide or do for themselves. In your notebook, list the actions of the will found in these verses.

Almost all the things we have studied, or are going to study, have to do with our *will*. Many Scriptures that do not directly mention our *will* do, nevertheless, imply the use of the human will. Here are portions of two verses that I have rephrased to emphasize more directly this *will concept* in them:

1 Peter 2:2: A new believer should be like a new baby. He should *will to drink* spiritual milk.

2 Peter 3:18: The believer should always *will to grow* in the grace and knowledge of Jesus Christ.

9 Take the following Scriptures and reword portions of them in your notebook. In your rewording, emphasize the *will concepts* by underlining them.

a Ephesians 4:15
b 2 Peter 1:6
c 1 Corinthians 13:11
d Ephesians 4:13

Have you completed your notebook work for the preceding exercise? That's a fine exercise! You will find that a good understanding of the *will* is important and that this extra long assignment will help.

Hebrews 12:1-2 emphasizes the importance of human will in the race of life. This passage indicates that we are to:

Will to rid ourselves of anything that would hinder our spiritual progress, and *will to keep our eyes on Jesus* in order to make progress toward spiritual maturity in the race of life.

If you rebel against God's will, you are exercising your will wrongly. Christian maturity requires submission of our will to God's will. Even Jesus had to submit His human will to the divine will in order to bear the cross (Matthew 26:39-42).

10 According to Hebrews 12:2, Jesus was able to die on the cross because of
a) fellowship of those around Him.
b) victories during His earthly life.
c) anticipation of future joy.

This is a good moment for you to reflect. Do you wish and will to become mature as a Christian? Pray that you will respond rightly to the situations God places you in.

Lack in Diet

Objective 3: *Explain why it seems evident that in 1 Corinthians 3:1-2 the Christians' own negligence had caused their lack in spiritual diet.*

There is a saying in many cultures that a man becomes what he eats! It is important not only how much we eat, but what we eat. Some foods contain things which produce only fat. Other foods are good for energy and strength. There can be no doubt that Christian maturity is limited by our spiritual diet. We have already looked at this to some degree in Lesson 3. The newborn Christian is to desire milk. But, in order to grow, the believer must move from milk to solid food.

Notice in Hebrews 5:12 that if the Christians were maturing, they would be able to *be* teachers. Instead they had a necessity *for* teachers. They could not yet eat solid food (digest the truth directly), but had to drink milk (predigested food). *Someone else* had to study the truth of God in the Bible, prayerfully learn from God, and then prepare his own mind and spirit to teach them on a level they could understand.

In Hebrews 5:11, the writer to these Christians says, "There is much we have to say . . . but it is hard to explain to you, because you are (have become) so slow to understand." The full teaching of the Christian faith is by no means an easy thing to understand. It cannot be grasped or learned in one day. A believer will often avoid teaching which is difficult. Similar rejection is seen in a baby. A baby does not like it when the mother stops the milk-feeding and insists on solid food. Yet the mother knows that for her child it is the next step for growing up.

You have proved your desire to come into Christian maturity. But that doesn't make it easy, does it? We will see in later lessons that for the believer *solid food means*: (1) moving beyond basic Christian principles to more difficult concepts, (2) learning to know the difference between right and wrong, (3) accepting responsibility, and (4) forming Christian character in his life. To do all this you must *look to God for supernatural help* as well as exercise your own desire.

11 In 1 Corinthians 3:1-2 it seems evident that the Christians should have been able to digest advanced spiritual food and that Paul, therefore, regrets having to feed them with milk. What was the reason for his feeding them milk (v. 2)?

....

....

12 Name first a human thing then a supernatural thing that work together to develop Christian maturity in the believer.

....

THAT WHICH HELPS OUR GROWTH

Earlier, we discussed the power to grow which is in all life. Then, in the first part of this lesson, we pointed out reasons why growth does not happen. Growth has its limitations and its enemies. We begin to grow by receiving Jesus Christ: repenting of our sin and confessing His Lordship in our life. We have learned that this is the process of being born again. Our new life is spiritual. Do you remember Jesus' description of this experience? It is found in John 3:6.

13 According to this passage there are two births: one by human parents and the other by which a person "is born spiritually of the . . ."

The Holy Spirit Our Helper

Objective 4: *Explain to a believer why he may grow in Christ through the Holy Spirit.*

It is important to understand how the Spirit helps us grow. You have seen parents help their children to grow by teaching them to walk and to speak, patiently helping them to mature. In a similar way, the Holy Spirit is the trainer for the new Christian life. The apostle Paul explains this process in 1 Corinthians 2. The Holy Spirit reveals God's secrets to us.

14 Base your answers to these questions on 1 Corinthians 2:10-11.

a By whom did God make known His secret? ....

b Who searches the hidden depths of God's purposes? ....

c What knows all about a person? ....

d Who knows all about God? ....

First Corinthians 2:12 says: "We have not received this world's spirit; instead, we have received the Spirit sent by God, so that we may know all that God has given us." What a statement this is! The Holy Spirit comes to help us know all that comes to us from God. We could say that the Spirit comes to help us to "grow up" to full manhood. He helps us become mature. Like our natural parents; He patiently works with us toward this goal.

Jesus was, you remember, born in human form through a direct act of the Holy Spirit (Luke 1:35). It was the Holy Spirit who helped our Lord Jesus Christ fulfill His human purpose. He was led by the Spirit to be the obedient servant of the Father (Matthew 4:1).

15 According to Acts 10:38, how was Jesus prepared for His earthly ministry?

....

When Jesus had to return to the Father, He promised His followers another *Helper*. The word "another" (John 14:16) means one like Jesus Himself. This is a very important promise, and we should study it carefully. The word *helper* here means "one who works beside us to help."

16 Read John 14:15-20, then answer these questions:

a How long will the Helper stay with us (v. 16)?......................

b Where will the Helper be while helping us (v. 17)? ....

17 Read John 14:25-26. Jesus promised His disciples that the Helper would make them remember
a) part of what He had told them.
b) all that He had told them.
c) more than He had told them.

It is important for you to read John 16:5-15. Stop now and do this. Jesus says in this passage that it is better for His followers that He leave the earth.

18 What reason did Jesus give His disciples in John 16:7 for His going away?

....

Jesus sent the Holy Spirit to the church so that the Spirit might teach us and lead us "into all the truth" (John 16:13). He will bring us into the likeness of Jesus Christ. In this likeness we fulfill the true destiny of man. The Holy Spirit led Jesus to fulfill His human purpose as the obedient servant of the Father. Thus, through suffering death and being resurrected He won for us salvation. The Holy Spirit leads us to Jesus' likeness, so that as His servants we may be a body that reflects Christ upon the earth. What a wonderful plan! We are a part of God's very purpose in the world.

The Holy Spirit Working Through Our Spirit

Objective 5: *Identify two opposing forces in your life.*

Objective 6: *Describe your part in achieving a walk in the spirit.*

The Holy Spirit works through man's spirit. Man's spirit, as we have seen, is his highest nature. It makes man entirely different from other created life. It is composed of personality and has the ability for rational thought. In a way, your spirit might be compared to a ladder. The highest and most god-like part of this ladder is your *will*. The will is the power of choosing or making decisions. Theologians call this "free moral agency." This means that God gives man a part in determining what he will become.

The spirit of man becomes a battleground when man refuses to let God's Spirit direct his life. Have you ever watched two people pulling against each other to possess something. It looks like they'll pull it apart. That is like the spiritual *tug-of-war* that we find in Galatians 5:16-17.

19 Read Galatians 5:16-17. According to verse 17, what two forces are opposed to each other?

....

Galatians 5:19-23 describes our lives first when human nature is in control then when the Spirit is in control. Human nature produces life as described in verses 19-21. However, when the Holy Spirit controls man's spirit, He produces an entirely different life-style.

20 Read Galatians 5:22-23. The qualities found in this passage are developed through *the Holy Spirit's control of our spirit* and are often called the *fruit of the Spirit.* List these nine qualities in the order that they are mentioned.

a ....   f ....

b ....   g ....

c ....   h ....

d ....   i ....

e ....

21 Through the Spirit's anointing, Jesus received gifts for His human ministry. Read Acts 10:38 again. When God poured out the Holy Spirit upon Jesus, what did Jesus do?

....

....

When the Holy Spirit controls our life, He will do the very work of Jesus in us. What a promise!

22 Read John 14:12-14. How does Jesus compare what whoever believes in Him will do with what He is doing (v. 12)?

....

....

Let's look at Galatians 5:25 which says, "The Spirit has given us life; he must also control our lives." Another aspect of control is the daily control of our lives, the actual surrender of our will. This is called the *walk by the Spirit*. It is the way Jesus lived daily in His human experience. We, too, can walk by the Spirit. Study the illustration below.

Many other things which help us grow will be dealt with in Chapter 6, but one is important for us to understand now: *We are born into a spiritual family which is provided by God for our help.*

23 Read Ephesians 4:7-16. Christ placed people as gifts to minister to mankind in various ways (v. 11). What was the purpose of the work of these ministers (v. 12)?

....

We must surrender our spirit—personality, intellect, ability, and will or choice—to the Holy Spirit if He, the Helper, is to make us into the likeness of Jesus Christ. In His likeness, we fulfill God's desire for us. We also fulfill our basic need for direction toward our spiritual goal.

self-test

TRUE-FALSE. Write **T** in the blank space if the statement is true. Write **F** if it is false. Then, change the FALSE statements to make them true.

... 1 Time has nothing to do with the believer's maturity.

Time has ....

... 2 We must will to rid ourselves of obstacles to spiritual progress.

We must will to rid ourselves ....

... 3 A believer who receives milk only of the Word will grow faster than one who receives solid food.

A believer who receives milk only of the Word will..............

....

... 4 The only source of complete knowledge about a man is his parents.

The only source of complete knowledge about a man is his

....

... 5 Galatians 5:25 implies that it is possible to have life in the Spirit without allowing Him to control our lives.

Galatians 5:25 implies that it is ....

....

MULTIPLE CHOICE. There is only one correct answer for each question. Circle the letter of the correct answer.

6 The writer to the Hebrew Christians criticized their slowness to understand by telling them that there had been enough time for them to
a) be teachers.
b) build churches.
c) have families.

SHORT ANSWER. Write in the proper answer to the question on the lines provided.

7 There are nine personal qualities of a life controlled by the Holy Spirit in Galatians 5:22-23. List at least four of them.

....

....

> Before you continue your study with Lesson 5, be sure to complete your unit student report for Unit 1 and return the answer sheet to your ICI instructor.

answers to the study questions

1 Lack of spiritual progress that they should have made during the time they had known God.

13 Spirit.

2 God.

14 a His Spirit.
b God's Spirit.
c That person's own spirit.
d His Spirit.

3 a) Satan.

15 Through God's pouring out the Holy Spirit and power upon Him.

4 Trouble.

16 a Forever.
b In us.

5 approval

17 b) all that He had told them.

6 Because they were slow to understand.

18 In order to send the Holy Spirit to them.

 7 not fail.

19 Human nature and the Spirit.

 8 Be on your guard.
Don't become occupied with too much feasting and drinking, and
worries of life.
Be on the alert.
Pray always.

20 a Love.
   b Joy. ˙
   c Peace.
   d Patience.
   e Kindness.
   f Goodness.
   g Faithfulness.
   h Humility.
   i Self-control.

 9 Your answers may vary a little but should be similar to these:
   a We must *will to grow up* in every way to Christ.
   b To your knowledge you must *will to add self-control.*
   c Now that I am a man, I have *willed to have no more use for*
childish ways.
   d We shall all *will to come together* to that oneness in our faith.

21 He went everywhere doing good and healing all who were under
the power of the Devil.

10 c) anticipation of future joy.

22 By saying that he will do what He is doing and greater things also.

11 Because they were not ready for the solid food of advanced Bible
teaching.

23 To prepare God's people for Christian service.

12 The believer's desire and God's help.

for your notes

Unit 2
Progress in Christian Maturity

Lesson 5

Motivations Toward Growth

Growing is an exciting and yet difficult task. I remember a child whose mother helped him plant some seed. She wanted him to experience the process of growth. One day he came to her crying, "Mother, my seed won't grow. Every day I pull it up to look at it and it isn't growing!" Small wonder, you say. Yet, we are often like this. Growth requires time, proper diet, and good soil. For the believer, the soil is our human spirit and will. If you cooperate with the Holy Spirit, your growth will be natural and continuous.

Parents and teachers often use rewards to encourage us to grow. These prizes are called incentives. *An incentive is something that moves us to action.* The Bible shows us many of the incentives provided for Christian maturity. Some are rewards we realize immediately as we begin to grow. Others are realized only after patient waiting. Yet, each of these incentives is important. This lesson is meant to introduce some of these Bible rewards to you.

lesson outline

Goals We Relate to Now
   Desiring to Grow Up
   Knowing Right and Wrong
   Receiving and Serving
Goals We See Further Away
   Becoming Useful
   Looking Like Jesus
   Preparing for the Final Test

lesson objectives

When you finish this lesson you should be able to:

- Identify motivations for Christian growth.
- Distinguish between "human-life" reasons for growth and eternal reasons.
- Point out some of the believer's responsibilities in light of the judgment seat of Christ.

learning activities

1. Read the lesson in this independent study textbook.

2. Do the exercises in the lesson development, referring as needed to the textbook. Check your answers periodically with those given in the textbook.

3. Take the self-test at the end of this lesson and check your answers carefully. Review those items answered incorrectly.

key words

cycle	liken
endeavor	option
equip	preparatory
eventual	seek
issue	ultimate
judicial	

lesson development

GOALS WE RELATE TO NOW

Sometimes the Christian is accused of being "other-worldly." This means that he thinks more in terms of heaven than earth. The Bible, however, presents a balanced view of things relating to both heaven and earth. It relates to the *here and now* as well as the hereafter. Maturing as a Christian offers wonderful, immediate rewards. The Holy Spirit presents them to us as incentives to move us on toward our goal in God.

Desiring to Grow Up

Objective 1: *Point out what kind of people God wants us to become.*

The parents of a growing young child who misbehaves will frequently tell him, "Don't be a baby!" I cannot imagine a child who would desire to stay at that level. Every individual wants to grow up as quickly as possible. To become an adult represents independence. It is a time for additional duties and privileges. Spiritual adulthood is a real *incentive* for Christian maturity. We have seen from 1 John 2:12-13 that the passage from "children" to "young men" to "fathers" is an important one.

The desire to be adult, and the fear of not growing should cause us to make several important decisions. We must be willing to separate ourselves from habits, speech, and behavior which are childish. Remember that Jesus commended a "childlike" spirit (Matthew 18:2-5). But there is much difference between being *childlike*, as Jesus meant it, and being *childish*.

First Corinthians 13:11 tells us to put away childish speech, feelings, and thinking. Perhaps our childish ways are most seen in demanding that people do things for us. This attitude shows selfishness rather than concern for others, and is always taking rather than giving.

Also, we must grow to a higher level of knowing: that of understanding. To understand means to advance beyond simple memorization in order to apply knowledge and truth to everyday life. A child begins by learning only to say words, but a man learns what to say and when to say it.

1 In 1 Corinthians 13:11 Paul says, "I have no more use for childish ways," and in 14:20 he tells the Corinthian Christians to be "grown-up" in their thinking. In 13:11, these childish ways are listed as *speech*, *feelings*, and *thinking*. How mature are you in these areas of life? Use this simple chart as the basis for writing a self-examination in your notebook. Then pray that God will help you in areas where you definitely plan to improve.

	CHILDISH	MATURE
Speech	Usually about oneself: problems, plans, actions	Often about things of interest to others
Feelings	React with joy, anger, or self-pity according to personal desire of the moment	Suited by reason that considers eventual results, express concern for well-being of the group as well as oneself
Thinking	Values determined by own desires for pleasure and entertainment	Values determined by ultimate effect on others as well as oneself, pleasure is secondary to duty

There are three great desires for our spiritual growth. First, our Heavenly Father longs for us to come into full maturity as sons. Then, He can fellowship more fully with us. Our spiritual adulthood will glorify our Lord.

2 Read again Ephesians 4:13. According to this verse, what kind of people does God desire that we become? Circle the letter before the correct answer.
a) Christian
b) Loving
c) Important
d) Mature

A second desire for our spiritual growth is that of the church and its leaders. The apostle discusses his concern in Colossians 1:28. He says that "we preach Christ to everyone. With all possible wisdom we warn and teach them in order to bring each one into God's presence as a mature individual in union with Christ."

Thirdly, because of their need to grow up, people desire their own spiritual growth. Maturity is completion of growth or full age. It is normal for all genuine believers to desire spiritual adulthood. Let us earnestly seek spiritual growth in order to perform special duties and receive special privileges (blessings) that require spiritual maturity.

Knowing Right and Wrong

Objective 2: *State how mature people are enabled to distinguish between good and evil.*

Have you watched a baby crawling on the ground? He will put *anything* into his mouth. It could be eatable, or it could be poison. He has no ability to judge between the right and wrong thing to eat. His play with objects can also be dangerous. A stick or other object can greatly harm such an infant. As we grow up, our ability to use good judgment develops. This type of development helps us to tell right from wrong. This is an incentive for the believer to grow up. He needs the ability to tell the right from the wrong.

There is a definite danger for believers who do not grow up. They often read or listen to false teaching. Because they are immature, they do not realize its falsehood. They are open to deception. Satan finds it easy to confuse the "childish" Christian.

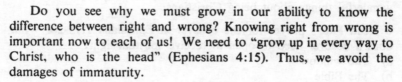

3 In Hebrews 5:14 an adult is described as being able to
a) become a father.
b) get married.
c) distinguish between good and evil.
d) quote many Scriptures.

4 Read again the passage in Ephesians 4:13-14. According to verse 14, children are "blown about" by every shifting wind of the teaching of deceitful men. What do these men do?

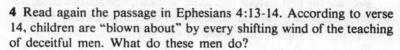

Do you see why we must grow in our ability to know the difference between right and wrong? Knowing right from wrong is important now to each of us! We need to "grow up in every way to Christ, who is the head" (Ephesians 4:15). Thus, we avoid the damages of immaturity.

The passage in Hebrews 5:14 tells us that it is through *practice* that mature people "are able to distinguish between good and evil." Our word "gymnasium" comes from the Greek word for "practice." As an athlete practices or exercises in a gymnasium, so we need to increase our ability to distinguish between right and wrong by practicing the right. We must grow up by the *practice* of God's Word, examining and doing things in the light of God's Word.

Receiving and Serving

Objective 3: *Explain how and why a believer receives spiritual instruction.*

One terrible thing about being immature is that we miss important messages. You often say to a child, "I can't explain this to you bècause you wouldn't understand it." Yet, children want to know "why" and "how."

This is the cry of the writer to the Hebrews: "There is much we have to say about this matter, but it is hard to explain to you, because you are so slow to understand" (Hebrews 5:11). The letter to the Hebrews was written to people who were in great spiritual danger. They were losing their way spiritually. There was a message which could have greatly helped them. But their immaturity prevented them from receiving it.

5 Read Hebrews 5:12. What lessons did these people still need?

....

Because the first lessons had to be repeated, new lessons could not be given. How sad! The full teaching of the Christian faith is by no means easy. It cannot be learned in one day.

The apostle Paul had a desire for the Ephesian Christians also. He wanted them to grow up. They could then REALLY understand the wonderful things about being Christians.

6 Read Paul's prayer for the believer in Ephesians 1:15-20. What does a believer need to open to receive spiritual light?
a)   The window
b)   The Bible
c)   His mind
d)   His eye

7 In Ephesians 1:18-19, what three important things need to be revealed to the believer? (List them in the order mentioned.)

a   ....

b   ....

c   ....

As we mature in this Christian experience, we are able to receive wonderful teaching by the Holy Spirit. The Word becomes very real, and it also is a means of teaching. The believer cannot afford to miss great messages from God through His Spirit and His Word, therefore he must open his mind to receive these messages.

8 2 Timothy 3:16-17 has an important message for us. In verse 17 we are told why Scripture rebukes, corrects, and instructs. Why does Scripture do these things?

....

God wants us to be mature and well-equipped for His service. This is a great reason in this present life for our pressing on to Christian maturity.

GOALS WE SEE FURTHER AWAY

Objective 4: *Describe the endeavor to which Paul likens the Christian life.*

Do you enjoy personal testimonies? I do. I especially enjoy hearing from older Christians. They have proven God's grace. Also, they are nearer the end of their life. They are soon to see their Lord directly. They see life from a better perspective. For many of us, the incentives we have just studied seem more real. But, the Bible clearly teaches both immediate and more distant goals for Christian maturity.

The apostle Paul testifies to the aspect of distance in the process of Christian maturity. "I have done my best in the race, I have run the full distance, and I have kept the faith" (2 Timothy 4:7).

9 According to 2 Timothy 4:8, what is waiting for Paul?
a) A prize of victory
b) Another race
c) A financial reward

Paul views the Christian life as a race. He sees the necessity of keeping the goal in mind. Have you ever been in a race or other athletic contest? The winner is usually the one best trained. We say, "He is able to go the distance." His body has been strengthened by exercise. As the

athlete trains for a physical contest, *train yourself to reach the more distant goals of a godly life* that require Christian maturity.

10 Read 1 Corinthians 9:24-27. What does every athlete in training submit to?

....

11 In verse 26, Paul says that he runs straight toward what object?
a) His death
b) Perfection
c) The finish line

12 Referring still to the contest of life, Paul says in verse 27 that he keeps something under control so that he will not be disqualified. What is it?

....

The phrase *finish line* means "goal." An athlete in training *must harden his body*, through physical exercise, for the race. The Bible prescribes both physical and spiritual discipline for the race of life: "Keep yourself in training for a godly life. Physical exercise has some value, but spiritual exercise is valuable in every way" (1 Timothy 4:7-8). The believer accepts hard assignments because he views the ultimate goals.

Becoming Useful

Objective 5: *Identify the goal of the Word of God in the believer's life.*

Usefulness may be classified as a somewhat distant goal. "But," you say, "isn't usefulness to God an immediate goal?" In one sense the believer is always available to God. The Christian life from the beginning is one of service. The newest believer can do a work for God. However, as we mature in God, we become prepared for greater responsibility.

At our house, the children are given work to do from their earliest years. The work assignment is to teach them responsibility. The quality of their work at first is not good. But it is good for them to work. As they grow, they do much better. They can be trusted with more important assignments.

13 Reread 2 Timothy 3:16-17. The goal of the Word of God in our lives is to qualify and equip us to serve God. What kind of good deeds are we to be able to do?
a) A particular kind
b) Some kinds
c) Every kind

We will spend an entire lesson later on the subject of our usefulness. At this point we simply need to realize that *total usefulness* is our goal. God equips some people to do some kinds of good deeds and other people to do other kinds. He wants to prepare us for *every kind* that He plans for us to do. Let us desire to become *senior ambassadors* for God, prepared for any assignment from God, trustworthy and ready.

Looking Like Jesus

Objective 6: *State the likeness into which the Spirit transforms us.*

Another goal is to become more and more like Jesus. The believer has an immediate desire for this. But this particular goal of Christian maturity is a lifelong process. As we have seen, this is the work of the Holy Spirit. The believer must choose to allow the Holy Spirit to control his personality, emotions, intellect, and will. The Spirit continually works at maturing the submissive believer into Christlikeness.

14 Review Romans 8:29 and rephrase it carefully in your own words.

....

To be like Jesus is an important goal on which we will spend an entire lesson in Unit 3. Here, we are discussing it briefly. Jesus Christ loved us and bought our freedom with His blood. To know Him and be like Him is both a daily and a lifelong goal.

15 Read 2 Corinthians 3:17-18. Isn't that a wonderful picture? We reflect the glory of the Lord! Into what likeness does the Spirit transform us?

....

To reflect the glory of the Lord, we must keep His beauty, His fullness, and His obedience constantly before us. Physically, mentally, and spiritually we must "keep our eyes fixed on Jesus" (Hebrews 12:2) in order to reflect a measure of His likeness now and a greater measure of it as we mature in Him.   What a challenge for an entire lifetime!   But we have much more to say on this in Lesson 8.

Preparing for the Final Test

Objective 7: *Explain how the believer is to do his preparatory work for the final test.*

There is a great incentive for the believer's maturity which is seldom discussed. Multitudes of Christians have almost no knowledge concerning *God's judgment of believers.* I am frequently reminded of a time in my college life when I returned to class after more than a week's absence. I walked in on the day of a mid-semester examination. What a shock! I hadn't read the assignments and didn't even know the area of material to be covered. But I had to take the test! That will be the situation with countless believers. Our Heavenly Instructor has told us clearly what is required and has carefully announced the time and type of examination. A consideration of these truths is most important for the believer today. It affects his priorities, motivations, and Christian life in every respect. May this study help prepare and alert us for the test.

Let's read the following Scriptures which describe this eternally significant event!

You then, who eat only vegetables—why do you pass judgment on your brother?. . . All of us will stand before God to be judged by him. For the scripture says, "As surely as I am the living God, says the Lord, everyone will kneel before me, and everyone will confess that I am God." Every one of us, then, will have to give an account of himself to God (Romans 14:10-12).

More than anything else, however, we want to please him, whether in our home here or there. For all of us must appear before Christ, to be judged by him. Each one will receive what he deserves, according to everything he has done, good or bad, in his bodily life (2 Corinthians 5:9-10).

16 According to 2 Corinthians 5:10, before whom shall we stand to be judged?
a) Christ
b) The church
c) The Holy Spirit

Please note carefully the following pronouns that I have italicized. In Romans 14:10-12 it is "all of *us*" who shall stand at this judgment, so that "every one of *us*" shall give account of himself. In 2 Corinthians 5:8: "*We* are full of courage"; verse 9: "*We* want to please Him"; and verse 10: "*All* of *us* must appear." These are the pronouns of God's family! It is not "they" or "them" but "we" and "us," the inclusive pronouns, that are used with reference to the body of believers.

One further thing of importance to discuss concerning our appearance at this seat of examination is the matter of option. Is it by choice? May we in some manner avoid it? Romans 14:10 says we "will stand," and verse 12 says we "will have to give account." Second Corinthians 5:10 says we "must appear." The words "will" and "must" leave no doubt about the certainty of our keeping our appointment for judgment.

We must quickly put away wrong understandings about this evaluation. This judgment seat has nothing to do with our salvation. In fact, as we have already stated, it is a family affair. There will be no unbelievers there. The original Greek word *bema* refers literally to a raised platform like that on which the umpire of the Grecian games would sit, and from which he watched the contestants and rewarded the winners. That specific seat was known as the "reward seat" and never had the concept of a judicial decision. This is not a place where the believer's salvation is reviewed. It is a place of inspection, examination, reward, and loss on the basis of life.

We have stated that every believer is called to be like Jesus Christ. Jesus lived His life according to the will of the Father and found His complete joy in that fulfillment. He took upon Himself, according to Philippians 2, the form of a servant. Believers are called to take on His image, to be His sons and servants. Thus we can readily see that this *bema* will be the judging of the believer's servanthood under the lordship of Jesus Christ. This will be even more obvious as we move through the Scriptures.

17 Read Galatians 6:7-8. This passage states a law of God which applies to the natural and spiritual world. It is an address to Christians that contains specific comments concerning Christian life and work. State the law of God in verse 7.

....

As we have seen, every farmer is involved in a cycle of buying, planting, working land, and awaiting the reward of his labor with keen anticipation. At great price, God has purchased and worked the soil of our lives. He expects results. Results will be a major issue in that day of judgment.

18 Read 2 Corinthians 9:6. Who will have a small crop, according to this verse?
a) He who sows little
b) A poor man
c) A city man

Now let us note two passages which were written by the apostle Paul to different churches, but which contain a great deal of similar teaching addressed to slaves and servants in the churches:

Slaves, obey your human masters ... Do this not only when they are watching you, because you want to gain their approval; but with all your heart do what God wants, as slaves of Christ. Do your work as slaves cheerfully, as though you served the Lord, and not merely men. Remember that the Lord will reward everyone, whether slave or free, for the good work he does (Ephesians 6:5-8).

Whatever you do, work at it with all your heart, as though you were working for the Lord and not for men. Remember that the Lord will give you as a reward what he has kept for his people. For Christ is the real Master you serve. And every wrongdoer will be repaid for the wrong things he does, because God judges everyone by the same standard (Colossians 3:23-25).

Actually these Scriptures are addressed to all believers. We are the servants of Jesus Christ. He promises us that there will be a time of reward for faithfulness, but warns us that we shall receive repayment for the wrong which we have done.

19 In both the above Scriptures we are to do our work as though we were working for whom?
a) The church
b) Our own father
c) The Lord

According to Romans 14:12 the believer must give account of himself to God. *Account* is a word which suggests a setting down of our blessings and opportunities to compare them with what we have accomplished: God's investment in us compared with our profitable return to Him. This concept is in 2 Corinthians 5:9-10 also. Look again at this passage of Scripture. It says that every believer shall actually appear before the Lord. At that time the results of his entire life will be reviewed. Evidently, this does not mean a recounting of sin. The blood of Jesus Christ, God's Son, cleanses us from sin. Sin will enter the issue only to the degree that it has kept us from being the profitable field, the worthy building, the image of Jesus Christ that the Holy Spirit tried to help us be. But let us not treat this point lightly. This will be a terrible moment. Concern over the "terror" of this moment should strongly urge the believer to do the work and will of God.

Even in this course, part of the incentive to learn is the examination or test. Paul clearly implies that being examined before Jesus Christ who gave Himself for us will be for some an embarrassing moment. It will be so particularly for the Christian who has received the grace of God but has produced no fruit.

Do you remember our study in 1 Corinthians 3? Turn to 1 Corinthians 3:9-15. In one of Paul's examples, he likens the believer to a building. Christ is "the one and only foundation" for this building. Thus every believer begins with the same foundation. The believer then begins to build upon that foundation. He builds with either carelessness or fine craftsmanship; he chooses his materials well or builds cheaply. According to the apostle, some use gold, silver, or precious stones; while others use wood, grass, or straw. Can we doubt the meaning of that comparison? Then the message becomes direct (rather than symbolic):

> And the quality of each person's work will be seen when the Day of Christ exposes it. For on that Day fire will reveal everyone's work; the fire will test it and show its real quality (1 Corinthians 3:13).

20 Now read 1 Corinthians 3:14. If what was built survives, what will happen to the builder?

. . . .

Take a moment to copy 1 Corinthians 3:15 in your notebook.

Here is a clear picture. Every believer begins his building on Jesus Christ, the foundation, when he receives Him as Lord and Savior. His building materials are shaped from attitudes, choices, priorities, maturity, carnality, Christian character or lack of it, things he does which affect God and himself, doctrine, use of finance, stewardship of possessions and time, words, habits, motivations, quality of his Christian service to fellowmen, and on and on.

The list seems endless. Every day we choose materials and add to the structure. But there will come upon us the moment of inspection. The examination of what we have built will be so severe that the apostle likens it to a test by fire.

Construction that is useless, careless, unchristlike, selfish, and carnal will quickly be consumed. Some Christians have so used their lives that when their works are tested, nothing will remain. Their works will be without reward. It will be as though they had never built upon their salvation. Others will experience loss but will find the fire powerless to consume what remains of true Christian works. These will be rewarded. And what better reward than to feel we have wisely built upon the foundation that our blessed Lord provided for us at the price of His life.

Actually every portion of Scripture that explains how God intends the believer to live becomes part of the evidence at the judgment seat of Christ. Colossians 3, Romans 14, and 1 Corinthians 4:1-5 indicate this. Perhaps you are now asking, "Just where does this place me? What should I do now?" Here are several points to consider:

First, it should not surprise us that such a costly salvation entrusted in the hands of men demands an accounting. Think or read through the parables of the Lord. How many of them concern servants left with responsibilities and eventually brought before their Lord for an accounting? Ask yourself this question: Does this scriptural review of the judgment seat of Christ make me more aware of my responsibility for having received such a great salvation?

Secondly, there is a clear implication in the Scriptures that the believer who is aware of future judgment can make changes in his priorities and life which will make the "examination" more successful on his part. For example, carefully consider the message in 1 Corinthians 11:31-32: "If we would examine ourselves first, we would not come under God's judgment. But we are judged and punished by the Lord, so that we shall not be condemned together with the world."

We can examine our lives now in preparation for the future judgment. We can change attitudes, review motivations, and redirect our energies toward the things that matter much in God's sight. Above all, we can remain open to the Holy Spirit who will guide us into fruitful, spiritual Christian life and service.

for your notes

self-test

TRUE-FALSE. Write **T** in the blank space if the statement is true. Write **F** if it is false. Then, change the FALSE statements to make them true.

.. 1 An incentive is something that prevents or blocks us from action.

An incentive is something that ....

....

... 2 A believer who does not grow up is often subject to deceptive teaching of deceitful men.

A believer who does not grow up is ....

....

... 3 The letter to the Hebrews shows that the Hebrew Christians could not receive an important message because they were slow to understand.

The letter to the Hebrews shows that the Hebrew Christians could not receive an important message because

....

... 4 The believer is set apart by God to become like His Son.

The believer is set apart by God to ....

... 5 A believer's salvation will be judged at the judgment seat of Christ.

A believer's .... will be judged at the judgment seat of Christ.

ALTERNATE CHOICE. When Christ returns and a Christian's works are tested, those which are eternal will remain while those that are only temporal will be consumed.

Write the letter **E** before those works that are eternal.
Write the letter **T** before those works that are temporal.

.... **6** Desire to develop beyond spiritual childhood

.... **7** Judging a Christian brother or sister

.... **8** Concern over the praises of men

.... **9** Ultimate Christlikeness

....**10** Living according to God's Word

....**11** Storing up riches on earth

SHORT ANSWER. Write in the proper answer to the question on the lines provided.

12 What is the name for the place of judgment and reward for a believer's work? ....

answers to the study questions

1 Your own self-evaluation.

11 c) The finish line.

2 d) Mature.

12 His body.

3 c) distinguish between good and evil.

13 c) Every kind.

4 Lead others into error by tricks which they invent.

14 Here is a sample answer:
God planned that those whom He already knew would be like His Son, so that His Son would be the first among many brothers.

5 First lessons of God's message.

15 Into the likeness of the Lord.

6 c) His mind.

16 a) Christ.

7 **a** The hope of his calling.
b The richness of God's blessings for him.
c The greatness of God's power in him.

17 A person will reap exactly what he sows.

8 So that the person who serves God may be fully qualified and equipped to do good deeds.

18 a) He who sows little.

9 a) A prize of victory.

19 c) The Lord.

10 Strict discipline.

20 He will receive a reward.

Elements That Build Toward Christian Maturity

What could a workman do without his tools? No matter how beautiful the plans for his building. No matter how wonderful the seed for his planting. He must have tools to accomplish his task.

Christian maturity, as we have seen, is a goal for the believer. The Bible provides us with many helpful motivations for growth. Growing up in Christ will enable you to assume adult privilege and responsibility. It will preserve you from being tossed and blown about as a child. Maturing Christians are able to receive teaching that the Holy Spirit has for them. This teaching leads to goals of Christlike usefulness. The growing Christian must be aware of the *final exam* which he must take before his Lord.

Reaching these goals is the problem. We must become a grand building of God. We are to be His fruitful field. Mature family responsibility is a position that must be attained. But how do we accomplish these goals? This chapter deals with practical steps for accomplishing them. The following outline presents human actions and attitudes that God can use as tools to bring us into the likeness of His Son.

lesson outline

Total Commitment to Jesus Christ
Growth Through Bible Study and Living
Spiritual Power of Prayer
Recognition of Servanthood Under Christ
    Sanctified Living
    Living by Will
Understanding the Ministries of the Holy Spirit
Cooperation With the Holy Spirit's Leadership
Relationship With Other Christians
    Mutual Help and Growth
    Sharing Faith With Others

lesson objectives

When you finish this lesson you should be able to:

- Describe the human responses needed to develop Christian maturity in the believer.

- Explain how Bible study and prayer help to develop Christian character in the believer and in others through him.

- Identify ways in which the Holy Spirit and the believer interact to help the believer grow in Christ.

learning activities

1. Read the lesson in this textbook.

2. Do the exercises in the lesson development, referring as needed to the textbook. Check your answers periodically with those given in the textbook.

3. Turn in your notebook to the chart you made in Lesson 2. Under the heading *Spiritual* write the Scriptures that seem most helpful to you for spiritual growth.

4. Take the self-test at the end of this lesson, and check your answers carefully with those given in this textbook. Review those items answered incorrectly.

key words

audience
direction
excellent
interact
lens
obvious
prevail

remarkable
response
sacred
tool
vital
weapon

lesson development

In this lesson I wish to share with you some simple, practical *tools*. These tools are the main headings of the lesson outline. They have greatly helped me in my own effort to attain Christian maturity. I would like to suggest that you write these headings on a card and carry them with you. Or perhaps copy them in the front of your Bible. Use them as a list by which to examine your own life. I hope you will find these tools helpful.

TOTAL COMMITMENT TO JESUS CHRIST

Objective 1: *Explain the relationship of our position to Christ's position.*

We are born again by the Spirit of God. This cannot happen until we *believe* and trust Jesus Christ as our Savior. We accept His sacrifice for our sins and are broken in repentance over them. But in addition we must confess with our mouth that Jesus Christ is our Lord. Do you remember what we have already studied in Romans 10:9-10? "If you confess that Jesus is Lord and believe that God raised him from death, *you will be saved*" (Romans 10:9, italics mine).

Kurios is the word for "lord" in the original language of the New Testament. In that day it was used of an important person such as the Roman emperor. In fact, by the time the book of Romans was written, each Roman citizen had to go once a year to the temple. There he threw a pinch of incense into the fire and shouted, "Caesar is Lord." The word *kurios* meant absolute king, unreserved ruler. When the Jews translated the Old Testament into the Greek language, they needed a word that meant "God." They chose *kurios* and used it where "Jehovah" appeared in the Old Testament.

Do you see how meaningful it is for a Christian to say, "Jesus is *Lord*"? This means that Jesus is king, master, and ruler. When we say "Jesus Christ is Lord," we are not just repeating a creed. We are saying: "For me Jesus Christ has a unique and powerful place as my Master and sovereign ruler. He is my Lord."

Now, please turn to Colossians 1:9-20. This is a wonderful Scripture which lifts up Jesus. Here we find that Jesus is called the "firstborn Son, superior to all created things." In fact God made the world through Him, we are told.

1 Read Colossians 1:9-20. Write the last sentence of verse 18 in your notebook. What position is Jesus to have?

....

This *first-place* position means that my desires, relationships, and very life must be second to His place. Jesus becomes a *lens* through which I see my world and my personal life. A simple way to say this is:

CHRIST CONSTANTLY IN COMMAND —— CHRIST COMPLETELY IN CONTROL

I receive instruction from Him by His Spirit. The Holy Spirit is in control of my life. Can you join me in the following prayer?

Oh, God, help me to make Jesus Christ, Your Son and my Savior, truly Lord of all my life. I open every area to His command and control. My heart is open for the Holy Spirit to work and give Jesus first place in me. May others see only Jesus in my life. Amen.

GROWTH THROUGH BIBLE STUDY AND LIVING

Objective 2: *State how the Bible can keep us from sinning against God.*

My Christian growth is directly related to the time I have spent with the Word of God. The Bible is the Christian's main textbook. It is your weapon, your map and guidebook, your daily food. The Scriptures will guard your spirit, give you light, and plan your life. We have already seen in 1 Peter 2:2 that new Christians should be like new babies, crying for the pure milk of the Word. We have further learned from Hebrews 5:11-15 that by use of the Word we grow up from babies to mature adults.

Let us look at some basic statements about the Word of God.

2 Read Hebrews 4:12. According to this passage, the Bible is compared to .... and it judges ....

The Word of God has a way of bringing cleansing to our lives. This is very important for growth.

3 Read John 15:1-4. Jesus uses the branch and vine to tell His disciples that because of His teaching, they can be
a) clean.
b) mature.
c) friendly
d) Christian

Psalm 119 is one of the most wonderful Scriptures about the Word of God. Almost every verse (and it's the longest chapter in the Bible) contains a reference to the Word of God. God's Word is called His law, His command, His instruction, His teaching, etc. Now is a good time to read the entire psalm, and then answer questions to help your understanding of God's Word.

4 Psalm 119:9 asks, "How can a young man keep his life pure?" We can keep our lives pure by
a) reading books.
b) going to church.
c) obeying God's commands

5 Look again at Psalm 119:11. How can we keep from sinning against God?

....

A simple truth is that *God's Word will keep us from sinning, and sinning will keep us from God's Word.* His Word will also provide direction for our lives.

6 Using Psalm 119:105 fill in the missing blanks. "Your Word is a .... to guide me and a .... for my path."

7 Using Psalm 119:130 fill in the missing blanks. "The explanation of your teaching gives .... and brings .... to the ignorant."

There are many ways you can study the Bible. Some read a certain amount of the Scriptures every day. There is one suggested study called "2-2-1." Beginning with Genesis and Matthew, this plan calls for two chapters of the Old Testament and two chapters of the New Testament, plus one Psalm or chapter of Proverbs each day. Another plan is called "Topical Study." This uses a subject, such as the Holy Spirit, and studies all available Scriptures on that subject.

There is another ICI course called *Understanding the Bible*. It is a good plan to teach you how to use God's Word. *Understanding the Bible* is a course in this same Christian Service Series. Perhaps that would be a good direction for you after the *Christian Maturity* study is completed.

Remember: Your Christian growth depends on God's Word. Through the written Word, God reveals the Living Word—our Lord Jesus Christ. You will grow in relation to the amount of time you give to God's Word, both in studying it and obeying it.

SPIRITUAL POWER OF PRAYER

Objective 3: *Describe the results of the believers' prayer in Acts 4:24-31.*

Prayer is talking with God. It is a privilege for the believer to have an audience with the King. Prayer is a powerful way in which a believer matures. Being with the Father frequently in prayer helps us grow more like Him.

The believer prays to the Father in the name of Jesus Christ through the power of the Holy Spirit. There are seventeen words translated prayer in the original languages of the Bible. Each of these words has the definite meaning of asking. Prayer can best be illustrated by a child talking to his parents. As the child matures, the level of the conversation grows. We could spend an entire book on the subject of prayer. Our emphasis in this study is on the necessity of being consistent in personal prayer life.

8 Answer the following questions based on Hebrews 11:6:

a   What must we have when we come to God?..........

b   Whom does God reward?..........

God has ordained that man can communicate with Him through prayer. It is a sacred privilege and a great responsibility. It is most important to understand that our prayer *does make a difference* in our lives and the lives of others.

9 Reserve a two-page section in your special notebook for *Christian Maturity*, and entitle it: "Promises For Prayer." For now, write in the following Scripture references, leaving room between them to look them up and write them in later.

PROMISES FOR PRAYER

> EPHESIANS 1:7; 2:18; 3:12; 3:20; 6:11; 6:18
> HEBREWS 4:16; 7:25; 10:9; 10:19-20; 11:6
> JOHN 9:31; 14:13; 14:14; 15:7; 15:16; 16:24; 17:1-26
> ROMANS 5:8; 8:26; 12:12
> 1 PETER 3:7; 4:7; 5:7
> PHILIPPIANS 4:6; 4:7; 4:19
> PSALMS 3:4; 5:3; 62:8

There are yet many more Scriptures concerning prayer, faith, and answers to prayer. Some of these Scriptures give us examples that are encouraging to our spirit and will teach us how the tool of prayer can become important to our growth.

10 Read the earnest prayer in Acts 4:24-31.

a Who prayed this prayer?..........

b What were the results of this prayer?..........

George Mueller, a great Christian in the eighteenth century, cared for thousands of orphans. Yet he never asked any man for support. He prayed and all the needs of the work were met. This great man of faith and prayer discovered that it was better to begin the day with the reading of the Word of God than to try to begin by prayer. The reading of the Word of God in humility and meditation brings faith and power and the *desire to pray*.

An old Christian motto says, "Prayer Changes Things." But we must remember that *Prayer also changes people.* To be used of God, we must learn the lesson of prayer. It is a lesson learned more by practice than by study. The Holy Spirit teaches us to pray. Don't worry about how much or how little you know about prayer—*begin praying.* Be regular every day.

11 Read Daniel 6:10. How consistent was Daniel's prayer life?

....

It is possible to pray anywhere and in any position. I can pray during the activities of life. It is, however, important to set aside times when you and the Lord are alone in communion. This is how you can be refreshed, made strong, and given direction for your day. Little prayer will equal little power; more prayer, more power; much prayer, much power.

RECOGNITION OF SERVANTHOOD UNDER CHRIST

Objective 4: *Use Colossians 1:10 to describe the life and deeds of the believer.*

Consistent Christian living requires that we recognize that we are Christ's love-servants. The word *consistent* is a very important one. It describes "agreement" or "harmony." Our conduct cannot be consistent unless it is in agreement with what we profess. Stated simply, we must "practice what we teach." We need to prove by our life the faith we profess.

12 Read Colossians 1:9-14. According to verse 10, how is the believer to live, and what will he always do?

....

The phrase "always do what pleases him" (Colossians 1:10) emphasizes doing something the Master desires before having been commanded to do it. Any servant does what he is commanded to do. But the love-servant, the believer, lives differently. He sees what he should do and does it even before being commanded. Thus, his life shows that he really means it when he says, "Jesus Christ is my Lord."

13 In 1 Chronicles 11:15-19 is a wonderful story of three of David's mightiest men. Read the story and write a paragraph in your notebook about *walking worthy of the Lord.* The Holy Spirit can use this story in your life. Please do not go on until you have done this.

Now, read Colossians chapter 3. If you are alone, read it aloud. This section of Scripture is a pattern for the Christian walk.

Remember our previous study. To have the likeness of Jesus Christ is to have His mind or attitude (Philippians 2:5-8). This means, as we have seen, acceptance of our servant relationship to our wonderful Lord. Our acceptance of this relationship is based on sincere *recognition of our servanthood under Christ.* This recognition produces not only enjoyable Christian blessings but also *Christian maturity that performs Christian duties. If Jesus is really my Lord, then I will do my duties gladly and to the best of my ability.*

Sanctified Living

Objective 5: *Point out how a believer's sin affects his Christian maturity.*

Another aspect of consistent life concerns *sanctification.* This is an important word. It refers to our special relationship to God's holiness. Romans 6 is a very important chapter on this subject. The underlying thought behind the chapter is: "Since God has saved us by His grace and mercy, we should not keep on living in our sinful way." The apostle teaches that we are to live as *dead* men to our old sinful desires. Our new life is to live for Christ.

14 Now read carefully Romans 6:11-13. Verses 11 and 13 speak about this death to sin and life in Christ. According to verse 13 we are to surrender our whole being unto God for certain purposes. How may these purposes be classified?

. . . .

A way for me to keep sanctified and holy is to be sensitive to sin in my life. God's Holy Spirit is always faithful to convict the Christian when he has sinned. However, Christians respond differently to that conviction. If something has come between a Christian and God, it will keep him from responding to the Spirit's conviction as he ought to. We often say, "The sun isn't shining today." Yet we know that the sun always shines. What happens is that something comes between the sun and us. A cloud forms and keeps the sun's rays and power from us.

The Holy Spirit is always faithful to convict of sin. But we sometimes allow pride, self, and excuses to cover the *rays* of conviction. If we choose to respond in humility to conviction, we have two wonderful promises in 1 John 1:7 and 1:9.

15 According to 1 John 1:7, that which purifies us from every sin is the

a) Word of God.
b) blood of Jesus.
c) light.

16 In 1 John 1:9 what is the one thing we must do and the two things God will do about sin?

....

How does *sin* in a Christian's life relate to his growth in Christ? It *prevents* that *growth* by blocking the way to spiritual maturity. If I am to be consistent—If I am to "practice what I teach"—I must keep my life emptied and cleansed of sin. Sanctified living is essential to Christian maturity.

Living by Will

Objective 6: State how we relate our wills to God's will in order to mature in Christ.

Truly consistent Christian life depends largely upon the use of our human will. God will not do for us what we must do. We have already said that the human will is the highest gift of our spirit. This is where we are most like God. Every Christian must have definite "I will's" and some equally definite "I will not's." God promises His help and power to support our decisions.

17 In each of the following verses of Scripture, state in your own words how human will relates to human action. (I have given you the answer to the first verse.)

a Daniel 1:8   Daniel willed not to become unclean.

b Daniel 3:18 ....

c Luke 15:18 ....

d Esther 4:16 ....

Philippians 2:12-13 says, "Keep on working with fear and trembling to complete your salvation, because God is always at work in you to make you willing and able to obey His own purpose."

These verses show us the cooperation between our part and God's part in our accomplishment of His desires for us. God wants our lives to have consistent growth, and He is willing to help us to bring about His purposes. *Through the submission of our wills to God's will, we experience increasing Christian maturity.*

18 Another verse for this area of our growth is Colossians 3:17. According to this verse, you should do in the name of the Lord Jesus
a) everything you do or say.
b) most of what you do or say.
c) only those things that are spiritual.

UNDERSTANDING THE MINISTRIES OF THE HOLY SPIRIT

Objective 7: *Relate the Holy Spirit's ministry of truth to the believer's growth in Christ.*

Since man is fundamentally spirit, *Christian maturity* is *fundamentally spiritual.* Spirit is man's highest quality. The human spirit includes mind, will, and God-consciousness. It is in *spirit* that we find the image or likeness of God in man.

19 John 4:24 points out that God is
a) like man.
b) Spirit.
c) eternal
d) kind.

God and man are similar in that both are mind, personality, and spirit. Thus, they can blend together and have fellowship. God is Spirit: the Holy Spirit. Inner man is also spirit. Man can only worship God through the spirit and truth of his own being.

We have already studied the role of the Holy Spirit in our life to some degree in Lesson 4. Jesus told his disciples in John 16:7-15 that it was a good thing that He was going away. Although this was shocking to His disciples, it was necessary to His sending the Holy Spirit. From that moment, believers were to "grow up" under the influence of the invisible Spirit—not the visible Jesus. Thus, increased faith would become necessary. Man is convicted of sin, shown the way to salvation, placed in Christ's body (the church), taught spiritual truth, and given power for service—all through God's Holy Spirit. The Holy Spirit is the source of energy for the Christian life.

Jesus Christ can only be revealed and glorified through the Holy Spirit, and it is only through this same Spirit that the believer can mature. John 16:8 tells us that the Holy Spirit will show people that they are wrong about *sin*, and about what is *right*, and about God's *judgment*.

20 What two ministries of the Holy Spirit to the believer are pointed out in John 16:13?

....

In the first part of the answer to the preceding exercise, the Spirit ministers knowledge of truth to the believer. In the second part of the answer He helps the believer to practice (believe and obey) truth. We must know truth before we can practice it, and its practice must be added to knowledge of it to develop Christian maturity.

21 Acts 1:8 teaches us about another ministry of the Holy Spirit. It is the work of
a) destruction of sin by fire.
b) inspiring us to worship.
c) filling us with power to witness.

When you have completed this course, you may be interested in doing an entire course on *The Holy Spirit*, or *Spiritual Gifts*, or the *Fruit of the Spirit*. There are such courses and they would help you greatly to mature in your Christian experience. There is not space enough in this course to cover each of these subjects.

COOPERATION WITH THE HOLY SPIRIT'S LEADERSHIP

Objective 8: *Describe the believer's cooperation with the Spirit and relate it to his spiritual growth.*

Turn back to the section of study on the Holy Spirit in Lesson 4 and review some of the truths in it.

Now that you have reviewed some of the truths concerning the Holy Spirit, we are ready to study Ephesians 5:18. It says, "Do not get drunk with wine, which will only ruin you; instead be filled with the Spirit." Here, the word "filled" does not mean as water fills a bottle, or a bushel of oats an empty basket. It is from the Greek word that suggests "to pervade or take possession of." The Holy Spirit is not a substance to fill an empty receptacle. He is a *Person* to control another personality—namely, the believer.

In Ephesians 5:18, the Greek word for "filled" represents a *moment by moment experience*. We are to be continually *filled or controlled* by the Holy Spirit. When we are filled with anything, we are controlled by it. This statement applies to being filled with love, filled with hate, filled with ambition, etc. We saw in Lesson 4 that there are certain evil works that prevail when human nature controls us. But the believer filled with the Holy Spirit will be controlled by the Holy Spirit.

Galatians 5:16-17 speaks forcefully to the necessity of our *cooperation with the Holy Spirit's leadership*: "Let the Spirit direct your lives, and you will not satisfy the desires of the human nature, for what our human nature wants is opposed to what the Spirit wants."

22 Describe briefly the fruits that we might expect in our lives if we allow divine nature to *control* us (see Galatians 5:22-23).

....

We can see that although the Spirit of God is within every believer, the individual believer must cooperate with Him by yielding to His leadership. If I completely surrender my spirit to God's Spirit, I will become motivated, energized, taught, and strengthened toward my goal of spiritual maturity.

RELATIONSHIP WITH OTHER CHRISTIANS

Mutual Help and Growth

Objective 9: *Explain why Christ placed ministers in the church.*

The individual believer does not grow up alone. Like the child maturing in a family, the Christian needs others to help him grow. We need the fellowship, encouragement, and contribution of others. God made us to need fellowship with each other as well as fellowship with Him.

23 Hebrews 10:24-25 contains commands about the believers' fellowship. Verse 25 states that we are NOT to give up the habit of
a) meeting together.
b) prayer.
c) Bible reading.

It is wonderful when there are many believers in our home area. Many Christians meeting together is often very enjoyable. But perhaps this is not possible where you live. Our Lord gave a helpful promise for even small meetings of believers: "For where two or three come together in my name, I am there with them" (Matthew 18:20).

There is a remarkable strengthening of our life when we meet with just one other person. When two believers pray and work for Christ together, they multiply their effectiveness. (See Leviticus 26:8 and Deuteronomy 32:30.) Jesus Christ sent his disciples to spread the gospel in a certain way.

24 Read Luke 10:1. How were the first gospel teams sent out?

....

There are many other passages on the principle of working together for God. See Acts 10:23, 11:12, and 15:36-41. When the Holy Spirit separated people unto ministry and witness in the early days of the Christian church, He separated them by two's, three's, and four's. There is an obvious reason for this: when two are together, they support each other. They encourage and help establish each other. It is scriptural to believe and ask God to bring one or more others to work closely with you in your Christian life.

Bible study *comes alive* when we can discuss and compare views with someone else. Our witness becomes bolder when two stand together. Life becomes more consistent when lived before another.

If you are fortunate enough to be a part of a good church, you are in a helpful setting for growth. God has put excellent gifts in the body of Christ to strengthen the believer. Teachers are a gift of God for our growth.   And even this course of study can help you mature.

25 Read again Ephesians 4:11-12. Why did Christ give ministers to the church?

....

....

In short, the believer is called to grow in the fellowship of others. *Koinonia* is an important Greek word that appears often in the New Testament. It means "to share, to fellowship, to contribute." Look up the following references: 1 John 1:3, Philippians 1:5, Philemon 6, and 1 Corinthians

KOINONIA —
TO SHARE, TO FELLOWSHIP, TO CONTRIBUTE

10:16-17. In each of these Scriptures *koinonia* appears. Fellowship with God; with one another, witnessing before the world, and sharing the nature of Jesus Christ—what a wonderful way to grow!

Sharing Faith With Others

Objective 10: *List four helpful directions for Christian witnessing.*

Perhaps no area of Christian life is more confusing than witnessing. Many times we feel the need to share Christ with friends. We feel guilty when we don't. The witness of our faith is both an *expression of maturity and a means for more growing.*

The first and greatest witness we give is our life itself. Second Corinthians 3:3 tells us that Christ writes a letter with the Spirit on human hearts. Everyone can know and read this kind of letter. In a certain sense it may be said that the believer's life is a Bible, the only Bible that some people ever read!

26 Read 1 Timothy 4:12 and 1 Thessalonians 1:7. What important word concerning Christians is found in both these passages?
a) Witness
b) Judgment
c) Grace
d) Example

There is an important likeness between conditions that keep humans from reproducing children and conditions that keep Christians from helping to reproduce more Christians. Let us consider some of those conditions.

1. Just as a small child cannot have a baby because of the lack of maturity necessary for reproduction, so immaturity in our Christian life will often prevent the effectiveness of our witness.

2. Just as reproduction demands union between members of the opposite sex (a union that the Bible says must be through marriage), so a believer will only help to reproduce spiritually when he lives in vital union with Jesus Christ as Lord and Savior.

3. Just as disease or impairment of vital body areas will prevent reproduction, so sin and careless living will affect the believer's ability to help to reproduce spiritually.

27 Now, read prayerfully Colossians 4:5-6. In these verses are four simple directions to follow in our witnessing. List them here in the order that they are mentioned.

a ....

b ....

c ....

d ....

Each of these directions could be expanded, but our space is limited. You may wish to list the following Scriptures in your notebook (under *spiritual)* for future reference to the subject of witnessing: 1 Peter 3:15, Matthew 5:13, and Luke 12:11-12.

When you share your faith, there is a strengthening of your own faith. *It is an activity that not only brings others to the Lord but also increases our own spiritual maturity.*

self-test

COMPLETION. Since our effectiveness for God, and our growth will depend on how we use the tools God has provided for us, maybe you would like to examine yourself on these points. Complete the following statements by marking S if your use of the numbered "tool" is Strong, M, for Medium, W for Weak, and N for Needs change.

	S	M	W	N
1. TOTAL COMMITMENT TO JESUS CHRIST				
2. BIBLE STUDY				
3. PRAYER				
4. LIVING AS CHRIST'S SERVANT				
5. YIELDING TO THE HOLY SPIRIT				
6. RELATIONSHIP WITH OTHER CHRISTIANS				
7. WITNESSING				

TRUE-FALSE. Write T in the blank space preceding the following statement if the statement is true. Write F if the statement is false.

... 8 God will forgive our sins and purify us from wrong doing whether or not we confess our sins.

... 9 According to George Mueller, a great prayer warrior, it is better to begin the day with prayer rather than the reading of the Word of God.

... 10 Sanctification refers to the believer's special relationship to God's holiness.

MULTIPLE CHOICE. There is only one correct answer for the following question. Circle the letter of the correct answer.

11 The word *koinonia* in the original language of the New Testament is connected with which important concept?
a) Spiritual as opposed to carnal
b) Fellowship, sharing, contributing
c) Growth through suffering
d) The plan of the Word of God

SHORT ANSWER. Write in the proper answer to the question on the lines provided.

12 There are conditions which will prevent humans from reproducing children that can be compared to conditions which keep Christians from helping to reproduce other Christians. List two of them.

....

....

answers to the study questions

1 First place in all things.

15 b) blood of Jesus.

2 a double edge sword, the desires and thoughts of man's heart.

16 We must confess our sins, and God will forgive our sins and purify us from wrongdoing.

3 a) clean.

17 a See example.
  b Three men willed not to worship heathen gods.
  c A man willed to go to his father.
  d A woman willed to go to the king.

4 c) obeying God's commands.

18 a) everything you do or say.

5 By keeping God's law in our heart.

19 b) Spirit.

6 lamp, light.

20 Revelation of truth, and leading into truth.

7 light, wisdom.

21 c) filling us with power to witness.

8 a Faith.
  b Those who seek Him.

22 The fruit of the Holy Spirit.

9 Your copy of these Scripture references.

23 a) meeting together.

10 a The believers.
  b The place was shaken and they were filled with the Holy Spirit and began to proclaim God's message with boldness.

24 Two by two.

11 Daniel prayed every day.

25 To prepare all God's people for the work of Christian service.

12 He is to live as the Lord wants and always do what pleases the Lord.

26 d) Example.

13 Your paragraph on walking worthy of the Lord.

27 a Be wise in the way you act.
  b Make good use of opportunity.
  c Use pleasant and interesting speech.
  d Know how to give a right answer.

14 As righteous purposes.

for your notes

Lesson 7

Foundational Truths and Beyond

Have you ever been lost? Perhaps you lost your direction in the woods, a jungle, or a strange village or town. You continued walking and, after passing a place you had already been, you realized your error—you had been walking in a circle. Instead of going forward, you were going round and round.

This can be true in our Christian experience. Many believers, as we have seen, refuse to grow up. Others can't seem to find their way. They want to go forward, but they seem to go in circles. There is a very important principle taught to Christians in God's Word. *We must establish what we have learned and then go on.* We should not continue to repeat the same lesson. Let us not linger in the child stage of our growing up. The foundation of our Christian experience must be made secure. Then, we must begin to build beyond foundational truths.

lesson outline

Maturity: Building and Leaving
    Seeing the Goal
    Knowing How to Reach the Goal
    Leaving: A Necessity to Arriving
Six Stones in Our Foundation
    Conditions for Becoming a Christian
        Repenting From Useless Works
        Believing in God
    Practices in the Christian Life
        Teaching About Baptisms
        Teaching About Laying on of Hands
    Pictures of the Future
        Resurrection of the Dead
        Eternal Judgment
Summary

lesson objectives

When you finish this lesson you should be able to:

■ Describe the process of the believer's spiritual growth.

■ Explain the functions of six foundational parts of the Christian experience.

learning activities

1. Read the lesson in this textbook.

2. Look up in the glossary the definitions to any key words that you do not understand.

3. Do the exercises in the lesson development, referring as needed to the textbook. Check your answers periodically with those given in the textbook.

4. Take the self-test at the end of this lesson, and check your answers carefully. Review those items answered incorrectly.

5. Review Unit 2 (Lessons 5-7), then take the unit progress evaluation on it and send it to your ICI instructor.

key words

doctrine	penance
foundation	require
guarantee	resurrection
ordain	

lesson development

MATURITY: BUILDING AND LEAVING

We have several times in our study come to Hebrews 5:11-14. Here, writing to a group of first-century Christians, the author discusses their immaturity. He wants to teach them important truths. However, the truths cannot be received because they have not grown beyond the baby stage. He tells them that it is necessary to teach them the first lessons of God's message over and over. They have not used the Word of God to grow. They will take only milk.

Seeing the Goal

Objective 1: *Describe the kind of faith that Christian maturity requires.*

Hebrews 6:1 continues this discussion on moving ahead. "Let us go forward, then, to mature teaching," the writer pleads, "and leave behind us the first lessons of the Christian message." Most translations read, "Let us go on to perfection or maturity." The word in the original language which is translated *maturity* means "a full age or a mature adulthood."

1 Referring to Hebrews 6:1, fill in the missing words in the sentence below.

We should .... again the foundation of turning away from useless works and believing in God.

What kind of progress could be made on a building if the workmen worked at laying the foundation over and over every day? None! It sounds funny just to ask that question. Likewise, no teacher can ever get anywhere if he must lay the foundations over and over again.

Great teachers in the era of the New Testament generally divided their students into three groups: (1) the beginners, (2) those making some progress, and (3) those making more progress. The goal of the believer is to be among those maturing: those who do not need the *first lessons* repeated over and over again. *This should be your desire.* You should want to go forward.

We have studied this goal of maturity from many points of view. It is to become like Jesus Christ, to accept our role under His Lordship. It is to grow in understanding. It is to be a teacher sometimes rather than having to be taught all the time. Remember that *Christian maturity*, does not refer to total or complete knowledge. It is not sinless perfection. *It does require a growing and responsible faith.* The longer we have known Jesus, the better understanding we should have of who we believe Him to be. The longer we know Christ the more completely we should reflect Him in our lives. Old faults should disappear. New virtues should appear and develop.

Knowing How to Reach the Goal

Objective 2: *State what the process of the believer's spiritual growth includes in addition to his own effort.*

"Let us go forward! And this is what we will do if God allows," so writes the teacher in Hebrews 6:3. Notice that this passage includes the writer. It is his own purpose to go forward. This is not just an exhortation to the Hebrews.

There is an important point which must be made from the original language in Hebrews 6:1. The word which is translated "Let us go forward" is from the Greek verb *phero*. It means "to carry or bear." Here it is in the passive voice and means, "Let us be carried along" to mature teaching.

Two important teachings come from this word study. First, *going forward* is not accomplished by personal effort alone! Christian maturity is achieved under the active power of the Holy Spirit. We have studied this in several places. The thought in this passage is of our personal *surrender* to an active influence. The power of God is already working toward our growth. We have only to surrender ourselves. We must yield to Him.

Christian perfection or maturity would be such a difficult thing if we were left to do it on our own. Instead, Hebrews 6:1 and many other Scriptures tell us that we are to be carried along toward this goal.

Have you ever tried to row a boat against the current? That is very difficult. In a way, the believer must fight the world's current. But in spiritual matters, the strong current of the Holy Spirit is moving on *toward maturity* for the believer. We have only to cooperate, by our will, with God's purpose.

2 According to Hebrews 13:21, who provides you with every good thing you need, and why are these things provided for you?

....

....

This passage explains further that an important reason for our going forward is that God may "do in us what pleases him." The goal is *our maturity and the glory and purpose of God*!

The second thing that must be learned from the study of *phero* in Hebrews 6:1 is that this Greek verb is in a form which shows a continuous action. "Being carried along" through the active influence of the Holy Spirit is a continuous and continuing action. It does not happen through a single crisis. Maturity in Jesus Christ does not come to us in a single moment. *This is vital for you to know.* The goal of this action of the Holy Spirit is spiritual growth into full maturity. In the same way, our surrender must be constant and continuous. We might translate this passage, "Let us continue to allow ourselves to be carried along toward the goal of maturity."

Leaving: A Necessity to Arriving

Objective 3: *Identify the things that the believer must make secure in his life before leaving them to go forward in Christian maturity.*

We tie a boat or canoe to a tree or dock so that it will not float away downstream. But we must untie the boat before we move away. Wouldn't it look funny to see someone rowing without removing the rope? He wouldn't be going anywhere! It is necessary to leave one place in order to get to another place.

Perhaps this illustration seems funny. "No one would be that silly," you say. Yet, in the Christian life this can happen. Every believer knows that he is supposed to move toward the fullness of Christian maturity. The full stature of Jesus Christ is the goal for his life. In spite of this, many believers are still occupied with the foundation. They continue to lay again the first teachings.

Notice the first sentence in Hebrews 6:1, "We should not lay again the foundation." Earlier in the same verse the writer says, "Let us . . . leave behind us the first lessons of the Christian message." The necessary condition to progress is giving up. As children mature, they must abandon old toys and other childish ways. Here, the word "leave" refers to moving from elementary lessons to a deeper knowledge, as those who pass on to a new subject or another grade in school.

But it would be foolish to build higher without first making sure the foundation is secure. The writer to the Hebrews makes sure that they will recognize their duty to progress. Recognizing this will make them anxious to see that the foundation is secure. Then they can begin to build upon it, rather than constantly relearn the foundation. In this study we will take a short look at the truths called *foundational.* Our purpose will be to let you establish them in your own life. They are not new, I'm sure.

3 According to 1 Corinthians 3:11, what is the only foundation which is laid for the Christian experience?
a) The Bible
b) The church
c) Jesus Christ

4 In Hebrews 6:1, things that the believer must leave behind are called the .... of the Christian message.

SIX STONES IN OUR FOUNDATION

Objective 4: *Define the word "catechism," explaining its relationship to our spiritual experience.*

The Bible clearly states in Hebrews 6:1-3 that certain doctrines are more basic or foundational than others. These are called the "first lessons" or in other translations "the beginning words" concerning Jesus Christ. The goal, you remember, is to go on to true Christian maturity. But we cannot hope to do this unless the sure foundation in Christian doctrine has been secured. A doctrine is *an important principle or belief of Christian faith.* In speaking of this foundation, the writer lists six doctrines.

5 Carefully read Hebrews 6:1-2, then list the six stones (topics) in this doctrinal foundation. (Carefully compare your answers with the answers I have given.)

a ....

b ....

c ....

d ....

e ....

f ....

Very old records tell us that the Christians in the first century treated these foundation stones as a catechism. *A catechism is made up of the elementary points of Christian doctrine taught to a new Christian to prepare him for baptism.* No one would suggest that these stones make up all the important early teaching for a Christian. Yet they are a foundation. You can see that these six stones are basically divided into three sets of two each. The groundwork is laid in becoming a Christian. The next two stones are examples of practices in Christian life. Doctrines concerning the future make up the third set. We shall study them according to this arrangement.

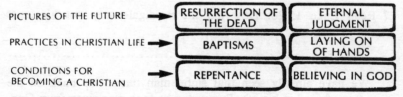

PICTURES OF THE FUTURE → RESURRECTION OF THE DEAD / ETERNAL JUDGMENT

PRACTICES IN CHRISTIAN LIFE → BAPTISMS / LAYING ON OF HANDS

CONDITIONS FOR BECOMING A CHRISTIAN → REPENTANCE / BELIEVING IN GOD

Conditions for Becoming a Christian

Repenting From Useless Works

Objective 5: *Describe the kind of repentance that is necessary to salvation.*

The first stone of our foundation conditions for becoming a Christian is "turning away from useless works" (Hebrews 6:1). This is an act of repentance. *Metanoein* is the Greek word for "repenting" in this verse.

This Greek verb has one clear, definite meaning throughout the history of the language. It means "to change one's mind." This is very important. Repentance in the New Testament emphasizes *decision* rather than emotion. Many people think of repentance as an emotion--the shedding of tears and so forth. Others think repentance is a religious rite such as "doing penance." It is possible to cry or to go through penance and not repent. Repentance is a firm inward decision—a change of mind.

The word translated *repentance* in the Old Testament means literally "to turn" or "to return" or "to turn back." The New Testament word emphasizes the inner decision, and the Old Testament word emphasizes the outward action. Put the two together and *repentance* becomes "an inner change of mind which brings about an outward turning back, or turning around." Through it, we begin to move in a completely new direction. This kind of repentance is necessary to salvation of sinful people.

6 Turn to Luke 15 and read verses 11-32. You'll enjoy this story. It is probably very familiar to you. Point out in your own words the basic *inner decision* that the prodigal made in verse 18.

....

7 Read Luke 15:20. How did the prodigal carry out his inner decision?

....

We have already seen that sinful man turned his back on the purposes of God in his life. Every step he took was away from God. Sinful man must change in two ways: he must change his mind and change his direction. He must turn from his sin toward God.

Read Matthew 27:3-4. Here Judas is said to have repented. The word here is not the Greek word we have discussed. It is a word which means "to feel sorry, to experience anguish." Apparently, he did not change his inner attitude or outward direction. The next verse says that he "hanged himself."

8 John the Baptist was sent to prepare the way for the coming of Jesus Christ. He preached a special baptism. According to Mark 1:4, what did he tell the people to do about their sins?

a) Turn away from their sins

b) Learn the ways of God

c) Become sorry and cry over wrongdoings

9 Read Mark 1:15. What did Jesus preach that we must do with our sins?

....

Everywhere in the New Testament, repentance is the first necessary response of man to the gospel. God demands it. You may want to write in your notebook some other passages that teach this. They include: Acts 2:37-38; Acts 20:20-21; and Luke 13:3.

It is important to note further that this first stone in our Christian foundation describes a certain kind of repentance or turning around. It is a repentance from dead or useless works. I'm sure you know that the whole world is "religious." Every person worships something. And there are very many religious "works." People hope to earn favor with various gods by religious works. These are useless dead works.

10 There are also works which produce death. According to Ephesians 2:1, what causes people to be dead spiritually?

....

Colossians 2:13 says, "You were at one time spiritually dead because of your sins." Man's acts separate him from God. While man's acts have a form, they lack the power to meet even the basic need of man—much less satisfy a Holy God.

Believing in God

Objective 6: *State what everyone who believes in God's Son will receive.*

The second stone of our foundation conditions for becoming a Christian is "believing in God" (Hebrews 6:1). Jesus said in John 6:47: "He who believes on me has eternal life." To believe is to place our trust and confidence in someone or something. Hebrews 11:1-2 tells us, "To have faith is to be sure of things we hope for, to be certain of the things we cannot see. It was by their faith that people of ancient times won God's approval."

One of the best explanations in Scripture of the importance to Christian life of *belief in Christ* is found in John 3:14-21. I know you love this passage. Many believers around the world are helped by it.

11 What will everyone who believes in God's Son receive?

....

12 According to John 3:18, why is a person judged?
a) Because of his sins
b) Because he is not a part of the church
c) Because he has not believed in God's only Son
d) Because he does not do the works of righteousness

In the original language the phrase "believing in God" suggests the idea of *being directed* toward. Our faith is toward God. The special tense or time of this word suggests that we are resting in that decision.

A great missionary was once trying to translate the Gospel of John into the language of the people he was working with. He could not find a word for *believe* in their language. (You know how many times *believe* appears in John!) What could he do? One day, a friend from among the people came into the missionary's house. He was exhausted from working under the hot sun. He fell into a chair and used a word in his language which meant: "I'm putting all my weight on this chair. I'm unable to hold myself up." Immediately the missionary jumped up and said, "That's the word I need." Was he right? I believe so. Faith means placing our entire weight and hope in Jesus Christ as God's Son and our Saviour.

Practices in the Christian Life

Our second couplet of foundation truths has to do with God—ordained practices in the Christian church. Some of these are called *ordinances*, or *institutes*. An ordinance is a practice that God has ordered the church to keep. For example, the Lord's Supper or Communion is an ordinance.

Teaching About Baptisms

Objective 7: *State the purpose of our baptism in the Holy Spirit.*

According to Hebrews 6:2, the teaching about baptisms is a critical part of our Christian foundation. There are many baptisms in the Scripture. They include John's baptism as a sign of repentance, the baptism of Christ, and the baptism of suffering. The Christian is concerned about three basic baptisms. They are: (1) baptism into Christ's body through the new birth, (2) baptism in water as an outward evidence of one's experience in Jesus Christ, (3) baptism in the Holy Spirit. A thorough coverage of this subject would take careful and detailed study beyond the scope of this course. A course in Christian Doctrine would be highly recommended for this coverage. However, through this course you will gain at least a working knowledge of this foundational truth.

13 Baptism into Christ's body through the new birth is the subject of

1 Corinthians 12:11-13. According to this passage, we have all been

.... into one body by the same ....

Underline in your Bible all the appearances of *single* and *one* in 1 Corinthians 12:11-13.

An important Scripture for us to remember on the subject of *the union of all believers with Christ* is Galatians 3:26-28:

> It is through faith that all of you are God's sons in union with Christ Jesus. You were baptized into union with Christ. So there is no difference between Jews and Gentiles, between slaves and free men, between men and women; you are all one in union with Christ Jesus.

The second baptism we need to know is easier to understand. It is physical. I refer to the believer's baptism in water. All Christians agree that baptism must be meaningful. It must not be an empty ritual (as would be the baptism of an unbeliever). When the believer is born again, it is an inward and invisible work. But the person experiencing this work is commanded to show it in a physical way by being baptized in water.

14 Read Acts 2:38. From this passage explain why baptism in water is necessary for the believer.

....

15 According to 1 Peter 3:21, baptism "is not the washing away of bodily dirt." According to this passage, what is water baptism?

....

No passage better illustrates what water baptism is than Romans 6:1-4. It teaches that baptism is an identification with the death, burial, and resurrection of Jesus Christ. The waters which we believers go into are like the grave. Through faith, we leave in those waters any remnants of our old life. When we burst forth from the baptismal waters, we relate to Christ's resurrection. "Just as Christ was raised from death by the glorious power of the Father, so also we ... live a new life." Again, I recommend that you study in more detail this subject.

The third baptism we should know is the one Jesus promised to His disciples: "John baptized with water, but in a few days you will be baptized with the Holy Spirit" (Acts 1:5). John had prophesied this in Matthew 3:11-12, "I baptize you with water to show that you have repented, but the one who will come after me will baptize you with the Holy Spirit and fire." In Acts 2 we read about the events in the lives of the disciples when they were baptized in the Holy Spirit.

Don't be confused because this experience in the Holy Spirit is spoken of in different ways. It is a *pouring* in Joel 2:28-29, a *filling* in Ephesians 5:18, *a latter rain* in Hosea 6:3 and James 5:7. There are specific passages which tell us of other believers (besides the first disciples) being baptized in the Holy Spirit: the Samaritans in Acts

8:14-17, the apostle Paul in Acts 9:17 and 1 Corinthians 14:18, the house of Cornelius in Acts 10:44-48, and the Ephesian disciples in Acts 19:1-7. *The baptism in the Holy Spirit is for the purpose of exalting Christ, producing spiritual gifts and fruit in our life, and giving us power for God's service.*

Teaching About Laying on of Hands

Objective 8: *Describe special blessings and responsibilities that accompany the practice of laying on of hands.*

Another Christian practice which the Word of God considers a foundation truth is the teaching about "the laying on of hands" (Hebrews 6:2). In Old Testament Jewish practice, this rite was used to symbolically transfer man's guilt to the animal sacrifice. It was also used to transfer a special blessing to a person, or to signify his being set apart for a special office. Practice of the last two of these forms continued into the New Testament. Let us briefly look at them.

Jesus blessed children by laying His hands on them (Mark 10:16), and others laid hands on people as a solemn means of blessing them in the name of the Lord Jesus Christ. People received the Holy Spirit when an apostle laid hands on them (Acts 19:6).

16 According to James 5:14-15, what blessings are given to a sick person as the elders of the church "rub olive oil" on him and pray for him?

....

The laying on of hands was also used to set apart a person for special work. Sometimes this is called *ordaining*. To ordain simply means to put in an official position or responsibility.

17 Read Acts 6:1-6. Who were being set apart to a special work in verse 6 by the laying on of hands?
a) The apostles
b) Seven men to take charge of business
c) Elders for the church

18 Read Acts 13:1-3. Who asked for two men to be set apart for a special work?

....

19 Name the two men in this passage who were set apart by the laying on of hands.

....

The Holy Spirit thinks it important that we have a basic knowledge of these three kinds of baptisms and the practice of laying on of hands.

Pictures of the Future

Now we come to the last pair of truths in the six foundation stones of our Christian doctrine. These are, "the resurrection of the dead and the eternal judgment" (Hebrews 6:2). These truths taken together emphasize the permanence of our present actions. They speak of the significance of our earthly life in the eternal order. These are the foundation stones which speak loudly of man's current responsibility.

Resurrection of the Dead

Objective 9: *Point out the guarantee that believers will be resurrected.*

There has always been a dispute in the world over any teaching about the resurrection of the dead. Even in Jesus' day, one group of Jews did not believe in the resurrection. It is a teaching that places responsibility upon man. Some men would rather not know that there will be a resurrection. Yet deep in man's spirit is the hope of a life after death.

The resurrection of Jesus Christ is very important to us. First Corinthians 15:12-28 is a section of Scripture that shows the relationship of our resurrection to that of Jesus.

20 State in your own words (based on 1 Corinthians 15:15) how Paul relates Christ's resurrection to our resurrection.

....

....

Let us emphasize what Paul says on this subject in 1 Corinthians 15:20: "The truth is that Christ has been raised from death, as the guarantee that those who sleep in death will also be raised." In Acts 4:2 the resurrection of Jesus Christ was being preached as proof that the dead will rise to life.

21 Read 1 Peter 1:3-5. According to verse 3, what is the believer given through the resurrection of Jesus?

....

Paul's dominant desire was "to know Christ and to experience the power of his resurrection" (Philippians 3:10). We, too, should want to know Jesus Christ in the power of His resurrection. Remember that in Romans 6:4 even our water baptism links Christ's resurrection with our own NEW LIFE. Praise God!

Eternal Judgment

Objective 10: *Explain why our belief in the sacrifice of Christ delivers us from the penalty of eternal death.*

Resurrection of the dead and eternal judgment are (as we have said) the last two foundational truths. Acts 17:31 is a verse that speaks very clearly about them:

For he (God) has fixed a day in which he will judge the whole world with justice by means of a man he has chosen. He has given proof of this to everyone by raising that man from death!

There remains before man the judicial process of God. It will be God's judgment through Jesus Christ.

There are at least seven specific judgments referred to in Scripture. They are:

1. The judgment of the cross where Christ, as a substitute, bore the judgment from God which was due the sinner because of his sins. At that judgment the substitute was executed. Thus all who believe in His sacrifice are delivered from the penalty of eternal death (John 5:24).

2. Judgment or punishment of the believer who persists in willful disobedience. We looked at this in the section on Wrong Exercise of Will in Lesson 4 of our course. Perhaps you would like to review that section. Note in particular the teaching from Hebrews 12. (See also 1 Corinthians 11:31-32.)

3. The judgment of Israel (Ezekiel 36:16-21).

4. The judgment of believers at the judgment seat of Christ. Perhaps you would like to turn back to the section on Preparing for the Final Test in Lesson 5 and review the teaching we have already given in this area (see 2 Corinthians 5:10).

5. The judgment of the nations (Matthew 25:31-46).

6. The judgment of the fallen angels (Jude 6).

7. The judgment at the great white throne, which is the place of judgment for the unbelieving world (Revelation 20:11-15).

These last two foundational truths are important to us because they help us live with eternal values in mind. There is no specific exercise involved with our study of judgments; however, reviewing the Scriptures referred to in this section will help to reinforce these truths.

SUMMARY

Remember that these truths which we have briefly studied are the foundation of Christian experience. We are to move on to maturity by not laying this foundation over and over again like children building, knocking down, and rebuilding in the sand. However, the believer must secure the foundation. We can't build higher until it is secure.

But once it has been secured, it is time to leave the foundation for other things. I believe the writer to the Hebrews is showing them that both Christian doctrine and Christian experience are necessary to spiritual growth.

The thief on the cross, the woman at the well, the apostle Paul, the Philippian jailer—ALL had definite though widely differing experiences. We too must know that we have had a real experience with Jesus Christ through the Holy Spirit. Doctrine is also important. There are many Christians, like Apollos in the New Testament, who teach sincerely but without sufficient knowledge.

We are to "go forward" to the building itself which is true Christian character. It is the life, the reflection of Christ in us, that really counts. This is a building above the foundation. It can be seen by people who may thereby glorify our Father.

self-test

TRUE-FALSE. Write **T** in the blank space if the statement is true. Write **F** if it is false.

... **1** If the believer is to mature, he must do it entirely on his own without any active help from God.

... **2** When the believer has established foundational truths he must leave these truths and move on, building on them.

... **3** A catechism is made up of the elementary points of Christian doctrine taught to new Christians to prepare them for baptism.

... **4** Repentance has to do mainly with an emotional feeling.

... **5** Doctrine is an inner change of mind which brings about an outward turning back or turning around.

... **6** An ordinance is a practice that God has ordered the church to keep.

... **7** There is no judgment for believers following their acceptance of Jesus Christ as their Lord and Savior.

8-13 The believer's foundation consists of three layers of two blocks each, as illustrated below. Please write in the order of presentation in this course the correct name for each block.

Pictures of the Future	12	13
Practices in the Christian Life	10	11
Conditions for becoming a Christian	8	9

Before you continue your study with Lesson 8, be sure to complete your unit student report for Unit 2 and return the answer sheet to your ICI instructor.

answers to the study questions

1 not lay

12 c) Because he has not believed in God's only Son.

2 The God of peace, in order that you may do His will.

13 baptized, Spirit.

3 c) Jesus Christ.

14 It is necessary because God has commanded it.

4 first lessons

15 The promise made to God from a good conscience.

5 a Turning away from useless works.
  b Believing in God.
  c Teaching about baptisms.
  d Teaching about laying on of hands.
  e Resurrection of the dead.
  f Eternal judgment.

16 Physical healing and forgiveness of sins.

6 The decision to go to his father.

17 b) Seven men to take charge of business.

7 By getting up and starting back to his father.

18 The Holy Spirit.

8 a) Turn away from their sins.

19 Barnabas and Saul.

9 Turn away from our sins.

20 Paul indicates that if we will not be raised to life, Christ has not been resurrected.

10 Their disobedience and sins.

21 A new life filled with a living hope.

11 Eternal life.

for your notes

Unit 3
Proof of Christian Maturity

Evidence of Christian Character

We are nearing the end of our study. This final unit will deal with evidences that we are growing into a position of Christian maturity. Several lessons back, I told a story of boys measuring their growth against a mark on the wall. The mark represented their father's size. It is normal and important that we have measurements to check our progress against.

The word *evidence* means "something that will furnish proof." Scriptures contain many clear teachings on Christian evidences. You know that evidence is often presented in a court of law. It is the proof of the guilt or innocence of the person on trial. A judge or magistrate or (in some instances) a jury of persons must weigh the evidence. They have the responsibility of judging whether or not the evidence is sufficient for a decision.

Someone once asked, "If you were on trial for being a Christian, would there be enough evidence to convict you?" That is a very serious thought, isn't it? In a sense the world at large is like a jury. Even unbelievers recognize whether or not the Christian lives up to what he professes or says. This lesson deals with the most convincing evidence of mature Christian life: the believer's manifestation of Jesus' character in his life.

lesson outline

Growing Up to Look Like Jesus
    Reviewing the Goal
    Characteristics of Jesus' Life
Being Like Jesus
    Choice of Will
    Surrendering to the Holy Spirit
    Type of Lifestyle

lesson objectives

When you finish this lesson you should be able to:

- State how the life of Jesus and the power of the Holy Spirit help the believer toward complete maturity.

- Explain how a victorious believer overcomes the difficulty that would prevent his spiritual growth.

learning activities

1. Read the lesson in this textbook.
2. Look up in the glossary the definitions to any key words that you do not understand.
3. Do the exercises in the lesson development, referring as needed to the textbook. Check your answers periodically with those given in the textbook.

4. Take the self-test at the end of this lesson, and check your answers carefully. Review those items answered incorrectly.

key words

character
enable
intimate
knowledge

manifestation
observe
victorious

lesson development

GROWING UP TO LOOK LIKE JESUS

Objective 1: *Identify our pattern for spiritual growth.*

The believer is born again into a new family, as we have seen. The newborn spirit (seed) within him contains the likeness of God. Like a baby growing into the likeness of its family, the believer should grow into the likeness of God. That likeness was seen in the face of Jesus Christ. Jesus was God living in human form. He set a pattern which gives every believer a model and standard for spiritual growth.

Reviewing the Goal

Objective 2: *Distinguish between partial and perfect (complete) Christian maturity.*

Let us clearly review the goal of our Christian growth. Romans 8:29-30 is one of the clearest pictures of this in the Bible:

Those whom God had already chosen he also set apart to become like his Son, so that the Son would be the first among many brothers. And so those whom God set apart, he called; and those he called, he put right with himself, and he shared his glory with them.

What we have already studied in this course has helped to define what it is to become like God's Son. In this lesson we are presenting the highest Christian evidence of all. This is the reflection of the character of Jesus Christ in our own character and life-style.

Another important description of the goal toward which we press is found in Ephesians 4:13:

And so we shall all come together to that oneness in our faith and in our knowledge of the Son of God; we shall become mature people, reaching to the very height of Christ's full stature. (Italics mine.)

Notice that the "knowledge of the Son of God" is an important factor in becoming a mature person. There are three basic levels of knowledge. We can know facts about someone we have not met. We can know a person better through having met him. But in a third and still more important way we can know a person intimately, such as we know a close friend.

1 Which of the three levels of knowledge do you think Paul referred to in Philippians 3:10? (Answer in your notebook, remembering that this passage was written from prison near the end of Paul's life and ministry.)

Now compare your answer with the detailed one given by your instructor. Hopefully, this heart-cry of Paul can also illustrate our desire to know Christ intimately as a means toward maturity in His likeness. We need to *seek* the most intimate knowledge of Christ as an aid to Christian maturity.

Paul was willing to live with *growth and growing* as a constant goal. In Philippians 3:12 he states, "I do not claim that I have already succeeded or have already become perfect. I keep striving to win the prize for which Christ Jesus has already won me to himself." Yet, a few verses later (Philippians 3:15), Paul puts himself in a mature category: "All of us who are spiritually mature should have this same attitude. But if some of you have a different attitude, God will make this clear to you."

This should greatly encourage us. The apostle Paul was able to say, "in one way I am mature. Yet, I have not reached the full purpose of my call. I am not yet perfect." We know that we can say of even a child, "Johnnie is a very *mature* seven-year-old." We mean that in comparison with the normal growth of seven-year-olds, he is mature. Yet he would not be mature compared with twenty-year-olds. Let us understand that we can be mature—growing as we should—and yet desire with all our hearts to come more fully to the goal of a total likeness to Jesus Christ.

Characteristics of Jesus' Life

Objective 3: *Identify traits of Jesus' character.*

Again, we say that our goal is the likeness of Jesus Christ. God intends for us to become like His Son. We can know about this likeness. Jesus Christ lived among us. (We have already referred to Jesus' life in human form.) He grew and learned and developed in His human role. He grew physically, mentally, and in favor with God and man (Luke 2:52). He accepted the role of a servant in order to fulfill God's purpose for Him. All of this we have studied.

Look back in Lesson 2 and review this material. Please do not go on until you have done so.

Our purpose now is to see what Jesus was in His character. *Character* is "the parts or features of our essential nature which distinguish us from others."

When we see a person's character, by words or deeds, we see the essential person. The children of God have basic characteristics. They may be from different nations, speak different languages, and have different color of skin. Yet, when true Christians are studied by an outsider, all of them will show the same traits. This proves that all of them belong to the family of God.

To study the character of Jesus would be a lifelong effort. I hope it will be *just that* for you. For this study let us simply call to attention several primary aspects of His character. The first trait we see in Jesus is His *selflessness*. He lived His life entirely to the glory and credit of the Father. John 1:14 tells us that as Jesus lived among us, "We saw his glory, the glory which he received as the Father's only Son." When men saw Jesus they saw the glory of the Father.

2 Philip asked Jesus to show him the Father in John 14:8. Jesus answered that anyone who had seen Him had seen the Father. What did Jesus say about His words and work in John 14:10?

....

3 In Hebrews 1:3 Jesus is described as reflecting
a) a borrowed nature.
b) earthly glory.
c) the brightness of God's glory.

In Hebrews 1:3 Jesus is referred to as "the exact likeness of God's own being." Even evil spirits recognized that He was the Son of God. (See Matthew 8:29, Mark 1:24, Mark 3:11, and Luke 4:41.)

4 Acts 19:11-16 implies that the demons saw God in Jesus Christ and in another teacher who was merely human, but who, nevertheless, was a godlike person. Who was this merely human person in whom demons recognized God's likeness?

....

In addition to Christ's selflessness, there were two prominent characteristics of Jesus' life that are patterns for us. Both of them are named in Philippians 2. This is a passage we have already studied. In it Jesus is shown taking upon Himself not only human nature but, also by a choice of His will, the role of a servant.

5 Read Philippians 2:5-11. Circle the letter before the two characteristics of Jesus described in verse 8.
a) Kindness and goodness
b) Meekness and tolerance
c) Joy and love
d) Humility and obedience

These qualities of the character of Jesus Christ are very apparent throughout His ministry.

We find many of the character traits of Jesus in a more indirect manner. As you read and study His life you see the characteristics of love, joy, peace, patience, kindness, goodness, faithfulness, humility, and self-control.

6 Read the story about Jesus' life in John 8:1-11. Now list three character traits of Jesus found in this story.

....

This exercise on John 8 is interesting. You can find many other Bible stories with which to do similar exercises.

The traits we have listed above are, as you remember, called the "fruit of the Holy Spirit." They are what we will produce when we yield to Him rather than our human nature. They are like windows of our soul through which God reveals Himself to the world. Jesus had all the windows of His human spirit open for showing the Father to the world.

BEING LIKE JESUS

Objective 4: *Explain why it is difficult for the believer to be like Jesus.*

To be like Jesus is both natural and difficult. It is natural because the very "seed" or nature of God is in us when we are born again by the Holy Spirit. This seed will manifest God's likeness as it grows in us. Paul expressed this truth: "Because of his love God had already decided that through Jesus Christ he would make us his sons—this was his pleasure and purpose" (Ephesians 1:5). It is difficult because "what our human nature wants is opposed to what the Spirit wants, and what the Spirit wants is opposed to what our human nature wants. These two are enemies and this means that you cannot do what you want to do" (Galatians 5:17).

Choice of Will

Objective 5: *Explain how the believer is enabled to be like Jesus.*

You remember that Philippians 2:7 says of Jesus: "Instead of this, of his own free will he gave up all he had, and took the nature of a servant." The spirit of man, including his will or volition, is man's highest gift. There is in every believer the seed of God's

likeness. Yet the believer must decide to let God's nature shine through. Ephesians 3:16 and 19 give important insights on how the believer makes this decision:

I ask God from the wealth of his glory to give you power through his Spirit to be strong in your inner selves . . . Yes, may you come to know His love—although it can never be fully known—and so be completely filled with the very nature of God.

7 Now read Ephesians 3:14-19. In the spaces below write some phrases from this passage which involve a *decision of the human will*. The first one, for example, is in verse 16 ". . . give you power . . . to be strong." (Don't repeat this example in your answer.)

....

....

....

It is God's wish (through the apostle) that all the virtues and characteristics in the phrases you have listed be ours. Again, however, the choice is up to the believer. A few verses later (Ephesians 4:1), we have the real issue described: "I urge you, then—I who am a prisoner because I serve the Lord: live a life that measures up to the standard God set when he called you."

There is a goal for the Christian life. There is a standard. The individual believer, however, must *decide* to live up to that standard.

8 What is that standard according to the last part of Ephesians 4:13?

....

9 In Ephesians 4:2 there are at least five character traits which we are urged to show in our life. They are marks of the Christlike life. Circle the five letters below for the traits mentioned in this verse.

a) Tolerance	f) Patience
b) Kindness	g) Humility
c) Love	h) Joy
d) Peace	i) Meekness
e) Gentleness	j) Longsuffering

This principle of the believer's *will* determining the character traits he allows to shine through is found in very many Scriptures. When you have time, go through the book of Ephesians verse by verse. You will notice how many times an appeal is made to your will. "You must put on the new self" (4:24), "So be careful now how you live" (5:15), "Put on all the armor that God gives you" (6:11), and so forth. For this study, however, we will look to one more Scripture. This passage shows us that God provides, but we must *will* to do something in our own lives about our manifestation of the character of Christ. It is a long passage but we will put it in the text:

> God's divine power has given us everything we need to live a truly religious life through our knowledge of the one who *called us to share in his own glory and goodness.* In this way he has given us the very great and precious gifts he promised, so that by means of these gifts you *may escape from the destructive lust* that is in the world, and *may come to share the divine nature.* For this very reason *do your best to add goodness to your faith;* to your goodness add knowledge; to your knowledge add self-control; to your self-control add endurance; to your endurance add godliness; to your godliness add brotherly affection; and to your brotherly affection add love. These are the *qualities you need,* and if you have them in abundance, they will make you active and effective in your knowledge of our Lord Jesus Christ (2 Peter 1:3-8, italics mine).

Now, reread this passage, noting the italicized words.

10 How many characteristics of the Christian experience can you count in this passage?
a) 8
b) 4
c) 12
d) 20

Notice in this important passage that the believer has the responsibility to add these virtuous traits to his life. Yet we are told that God has given us "precious gifts" and the "divine nature" itself. You see it is a cooperation between us and God's gift within us. *The power to be like God is realized through our new birth and our own free will.* We must *do* something to become like Jesus Christ.

This balance between God's gift and our work is seen in another important Scripture: "Keep on working with fear and trembling to complete your salvation, because God is always at work in you to make you willing and able to obey his own purpose" (Philippians 2:12-13).

Salvation can best be described as wholeness: the completion of the plan of God for each person. We must work, but God must make us willing and able. Praise God for that wonderful balance!

Surrendering to the Holy Spirit

Objective 6: *Relate the believer's surrender to the Spirit to his being like Jesus.*

We have studied the ministry of the Holy Spirit in Lessons 4 and 6. You remember that it was the Holy Spirit who enabled Jesus to fulfill the purpose of His human role. Jesus was led and anointed of the Spirit. The beautiful character of Jesus can only be ours through the Spirit's control of our life. The apostle Paul writes to the Galatians: "The Spirit has given us life; he must also control our lives" (Galatians 5:25).

When the Holy Spirit is in control of the believer's life, He will produce the character of Christ in it. This chart will help you visualize the nine *windows* of Galatians 5:22-23 through which Christian character is seen.

WINDOWS OF GALATIANS 5:22-23

LOVE	JOY	PEACE
PATIENCE	KINDNESS	GOODNESS
FAITHFULNESS	HUMILITY	SELF-CONTROL

11 Write in this space the positive command to us in Ephesians 5:18.

....

Remember that to be filled means "to be under the control or influence of." *The more we let God's Spirit control our life the more like Jesus we will be in character and life.* Sometime, read through the book of Acts and underline each place that tells of someone's being filled with the Holy Spirit. What a privilege!

Type of Lifestyle

Objective 7: *State who produces in submissive believers the spiritual growth that develops from attitudes described in the beatitudes.*

One day Jesus went up a hill and sat down to teach the crowd that had gathered (see Matthew 5:1-2). This teaching has been called, by generations of Christians, "The Sermon on the Mount." Included in this wonderful sermon are brief statements called *beatitudes*. *Beatitude* is a word which means "the utmost happiness or bliss." What Jesus described in these short statements was a type of living which would be truly happy.

Each of the beatitudes in Matthew 5:3-10 describes an attitude of heart and character which the Holy Spirit will produce in believers who allow Him to do so. These attitudes produce spiritual growth. Let us briefly observe them in a spirit of self-examination to see how completely we have submitted our hearts to the Holy Spirit.

"Happy are those who know they are spiritually poor" (v. 3). The Holy Spirit will help us to be constantly aware of our need. This attitude of dependency on God will produce rich rewards.

"Happy are those who mourn" (v. 4). This refers to an attitude of sorrow concerning anything that will keep Christ from being glorified in our life. It is the *godly sorrow* of confession and repentance.

"Happy are those who are humble" (v. 5). The very nature and attitude of Jesus shows humility and submission to the will of God. Humility is the most easily recognized characteristic of a servant of Christ.

"Happy are those whose greatest desire is to do what God requires" (v. 6). This is the quality of obedience. Just as Jesus said, so must the believer say: "Here I am, to do your will, O God" (Hebrews 10:7).

"Happy are those who are merciful to others" (v. 7). Here is the outgiving attitude of the forgiveness and grace of God. There can be no keeping bitterness and resentfulness in the heart. Again, this is an obvious quality of Christ's life.

"Happy are the pure in heart," (v. 8). If the inner heart is not much occupied with desires of human nature, your vision of Jesus' reality will be greater.

"Happy are those who work for peace" (v. 9). Here is the characteristic of a sharing spirit that pours out concern and compassion to others.

"Happy are those who are persecuted because they do what God requires" (v. 10). Here is the quality of rejoicing in all things. The believer can recognize the Father's loving hand and care in every step and experience.

12 Now, as you read through Matthew 5:3-10 again, write in your notebook the part of each verse that shows how God will reward the people who are described by each beatitude. (I have written that part of verse 3 for you as an example.) Verse 3: The Kingdom of heaven belongs to them.

The evidence that most proves a man to be a mature Christian is the character of Christ in his life. The Bible tells us that believers were first called Christians in the city of Antioch (Acts 11:26). Up to that time and for several more years, they were simply known as "the people of the Way." Antioch was the slave capital of the world. Slaves bore their master's name plus the ending "-ian." Perhaps the unbelieving world saw these people as "slaves of Christ." Whether or not that is true, there is no greater honor than being called a Christian. We *know* that Christian refers to "a servant of the Lord Jesus Christ." It means being conformed to His very likeness and nature.

self-test

TRUE-FALSE.   Write **T** in the blank space if the statement is true. Write **F** if it is false.

... **1** Evidence means something that furnishes proof.

... **2** Knowledge of God's Word is necessary to become a mature Christian.

... **3** The apostle Paul claimed to have already succeeded and become perfect.

... **4** Character is the parts or features of our essential nature which distinguish us from others.

... **5** The beatitudes describe attitudes of heart and character that the Holy Spirit will produce in the believer.

SHORT ANSWER. Write in the proper answer to the questions on the lines provided.

6 Place an X beside the fruits of the Spirit that are found in Galatians 5:22-23.

... a) Goodness   ... f) Patience   ... k) Humility

... b) Miracles   ... g) Kindness   ... l) Self-control

... c) Peace   ... h) Faith   ... m) Love

... d) Being   ... i) Healings   ... n) Wisdom

... e) Tongues   ... j) Faithfulness   ... o) Joy

7 Since the character of Christ in our life is an evidence of Christian maturity, perhaps you would like to evaluate yourself on the following characteristics. Check **S** for strong, **M** for medium, **W** for weak, and **N** for need to grow.

Characteristics	S	M	W	N
Love				
Joy				
Peace				
Patience				
Kindness				
Goodness				
Faithfulness				
Humility				
Self-control				
Knowledge				
Godliness				

answers to the study questions

1 Paul referred to the third or intimate level. He knew the facts of Jesus Christ (Galatians 1:6-10). He knew Christ through personal experience (Acts 9:1-19). But the desire to know the Lord intimately is a lifelong desire which will only be completely fulfilled in the Lord's presence in eternity.

7 "through faith" (v. 17), "you may have your roots and foundation in love" (v. 17), "you . . . may have the power to understand" (v. 18), "may you come to know" (v. 19).

2 That they came from the Father.

8 The very height of Christ's full stature.

3 c) the brightness of God's glory.

9 a) Tolerance.
c) Love.
e) Gentleness.
f) Patience.
g) Humility.

4 Paul.

10 a) 8.

5 d) Humility and obedience.

11 Be filled with the Spirit.

6 Kindness, love, and gentleness. (Other traits of Jesus may be found here.)

12 Verse   3: The Kingdom of heaven belongs to them.
Verse   4: God will comfort them.
Verse   5: They will receive what God has promised.
Verse   6: God will satisfy them fully.
Verse   7: God will be merciful to them.
Verse   8: They will see God!
Verse   9: God will call them His children.
Verse 10: The Kingdom of heaven belongs to them.

Lesson 9

Evidence of Useful Ministry

We have seen Christian maturity as the normal process of growth. It can be hindered and stopped by enemies of maturity inside and outside the believer. Yet, there are great and wonderful things which work to bring him to maturity. "The Spirit who is in you is more powerful than the spirit in those who belong to the world" (1 John 4:4).

There are specific evidences in a believer who is moving toward the image of Jesus Christ. First, he bears the unmistakable family resemblance. He begins more and more to express the character of Jesus Christ in his habits, and attitudes. The world says to the church, "Sir, we want to see Jesus" (John 12:21). The maturing believer is an answer to the world. Men and women under the control of the Holy Spirit manifest the life and likeness of Jesus Christ. The world can see Jesus in us!

The believer's work is a second and equally clear evidence of maturity. A growing believer is a useful believer. As maturity increases, the believer becomes more and more able to accept responsibility. His assignments in Christian service become more important. One of the greatest thrills a father and mother have is to see their child grow to a point of usefulness. They are thrilled to see their child do his first tasks and learned his first craft. It is a mark of real achievement when the growing person becomes responsible and useful. Useful ministry is a real evidence of Christian maturity. It is proof that we are coming to our goal as believers.

lesson outline

Christ's Ministry
    Christ's Example of Usefulness
    The Father's Glory
The Believer's Ministry
    Fulfilling Jesus' Ministry
    Showing Maturity Through Works
    Continuing by the Holy Spirit
Summary

lesson objectives

When you finish this lesson you should be able to:

■ Understand more fully the value of Jesus' useful ministry.

■ Relate Jesus' ministry to the believer's ministry.

learning activities

1. Read the lesson in this textbook.

2. Do the exercises in the lesson development, referring as needed to the textbook. Check your answers periodically with those given in the textbook.

3. Take the self-test at the end of this lesson, and check your answers carefully. Review those items answered incorrectly.

key words

commend	qualification
equipped	redeem
glorify	reminder
paralyzed	

lesson development

Originally, God gave man a useful ministry. Our earliest glimpse of man is of his usefulness in the Garden of Eden. He is working there. "Then the Lord God placed the man in the Garden of Eden to cultivate it and guard it" (Genesis 2:15). God is shown throughout the Scriptures as creating the world and working in it. When God made man he said, "Now we will make human beings; they will be like us and resemble us. They will have power over the fish, the birds, and all animals, domestic and wild, large and small" (Genesis 1:26). God further commanded that men should live all over the earth and would "bring it under their control." God said, "I am putting you in charge" (Genesis 1:28). At this point, as we saw in Lesson 1, God could say that *He was very pleased* with all that He had made.

Then sin, as we have seen, interfered with man's achieving his full ministry under God. Man was driven from the Garden of Eden and from his place of shared dominion over the earth. But there was still to be work for man. Concerning the ground God told Adam, "You will have to work hard all your life to make it produce enough food for you ... You will have to work hard and sweat to make the soil produce anything" (Genesis 3:17-19).

Thank God that through Jesus Christ, man can be redeemed from sin by faith! Through the power of the Holy Spirit, he can again do the useful works that God intended for him to do. The pattern for our useful ministry is Jesus Himself.

CHRIST'S MINISTRY

Christ's Example of Usefulness

Objective 1: *State the witness on behalf of Jesus that is greater than the witness that John the Baptist gave.*

In the second book that Luke wrote, called "The Acts of the Apostles" in our Bible, he begins: "In my first book I wrote about all the things that Jesus did and taught from the time he began his work" (Acts 1:1). Later in his second book, Luke emphasizes the *usefulness* of Jesus' work: "He went everywhere, doing good" (Acts 10:38).

Early in His ministry, Jesus healed a paralyzed man on the Sabbath. Then Jewish authorities began to persecute Him because He had done this healing on a Sabbath. Jesus answered them, "My Father is always working, and I too must work" (John 5:17). This is a specific example of the usefulness of Jesus' work.

1 According to John 5:36, what is the greater witness on behalf of Jesus than the witness that John the Baptist gave?
a) Jesus' miraculous power
b) Jesus' acceptance of common people
c) Jesus' works

2 Answer these questions based on John 9:4.
a How long does Jesus say the work must continue?

....

b When does He say His work will stop?

....

The Father's Glory

Objective 2: *Explain the relationship between Jesus' work and the Father's glory.*

Jesus would do nothing against the Father's will. His life was lived entirely to accomplish the Father's purpose. He once said, "My food . . . is to obey the will of the one who sent me and to finish the work he gave me to do" (John 4:34). He was able to say to everyone that His works, His life, and His words were all the Father's. At the end of Jesus' life, He could tell the Father, "I have shown your glory on earth; I have finished the work you gave me to do" (John 17:4). This verse in *The New International Version* reads: "I have brought you glory on earth by completing the work you gave me to do."

3 According to Jesus' words in John 10:25, what is it that will speak on His behalf?

....

4 According to John 17:4, why did Jesus' work bring glory to the Father?

....

THE BELIEVER'S MINISTRY

The believer's maturity, as we have seen, is measured by the standard of the full stature of Jesus Christ. One clear measurement is therefore the character of Christ in the believer. Another, and no less important, evidence of Christian maturity is the ministry of Jesus Christ accomplished by the believer through the Holy Spirit.

Fulfilling Jesus' Ministry

Objective 3: *State how the ministry of Jesus is being fulfilled in the world now.*

In John 14:12-14 Jesus declared an important truth about the believer's ministry:

I am telling you the truth: whoever believes in me will do what I do—yes, he will do even greater things, because I am going to the Father. And I will do whatever you ask for in my name, so that the Father's glory will be shown through the Son. If you ask me for anything in my name, I will do it.

Do you understand this word from Jesus? The believer will give proof of Christian maturity by doing the works which Jesus did. These works will *glorify* the Father as did the works of Jesus Himself.

5 How is the ministry of Jesus being fulfilled in the world now?

....

We have seen in our earlier study that the subject of maturity in the Bible is sometimes compared to farming. Jesus used this illustration in a powerful teaching. It concerns the believer's ministry. Jesus said, "I chose you and appointed you to go and bear much fruit, the kind of fruit that endures" (John 15:16). In this important teaching Jesus stated that he is the real vine and the Father is the gardener. The believer is a branch which can only bear fruit as it remains in union with the vine.

6 According to John 15:7, what is the condition that the believer must fulfill in order to get what he asks Jesus for?

....

7 According to John 15:10, what must the believer do in order to remain in Jesus' love?

....

The believer's fruitfulness is an evidence of his ministry. But each believer must remember that his ministry is a fulfillment of Jesus' ministry. The believer "can do nothing" without Him (John 15:5).

Showing Maturity Through Works

Objective 4: *Explain how the seven men chosen in Acts 6: 1-7 showed evidence of their maturity.*

We have studied the tragic lack of usefulness which is a sign of immaturity. The writer to the Hebrews complains: "There has been enough time for you to be teachers—yet you still need someone to teach you the first lessons of God's message" (Hebrews 5:12). He was looking for the evidence of Christian maturity. Growing Christians were meant to be useful. The ministry of teaching was the evidence he was looking for. A very important Scripture on this subject is 2 Timothy 3:16-17:

All Scripture is inspired by God and is useful for teaching
the truth, rebuking error, correcting faults, and giving

instruction for right living, so that the person who serves God may be *fully qualified and equipped* to do every kind of good deed (italics mine).

I have italicized "fully qualified and equipped" because in the original language these words express the idea of maturity. You remember that the word *mature* means "to bring to completion," or to furnish and equip. God's purpose is to bring us to a point of maturity or completion through His Word. Then we will be able to do works which glorify Him. Again, the good deeds which follow will be evidence that we have been "fully qualified" to do them, and that we are maturing in Jesus Christ.

8 Read Acts 6:1-7 carefully. There was a great need in the church. To take care of this need, the apostles ordered the church to select seven men who were mature for service. In Acts 6:3 two evidences of maturity are stated as necessary qualifications in the lives of those to be chosen. Indicate these evidences by completing the following statement.

These seven men were to be full of .... and ....

9 Then seven mature men were put in charge of the matter that had caused the need in the church (Acts 6:1-7). How did these men show evidence of their maturity?

....

Because these seven men were mature, growing Christians, they could be put in charge of the matter that had caused the need. Usefulness to the church was an evidence of their Christian maturity.

In Colossians 1, considered earlier, the apostle Paul tells of his prayers for those early Christians:

For this reason we have always prayed for you, ever since we heard about you. We ask God to fill you with the knowledge of His will, with all the wisdom and understanding that His Spirit gives. Then you will be able to live as the Lord wants and will always do what pleases Him. Your lives will produce all kinds of good deeds, and you will grow in your knowledge of God (Colossians 1:9-10).

10 In Colossians 1:10, what is an evidence that the believer is in a place where his life is one that pleases the Lord? (Each answer may seem right, but look carefully at the Scripture and choose your answer from it.)

a) That the believer is maturing in general.
b) That the believer does not sin any longer.
c) That the believer's life will produce good deeds.
d) That the believer always fellowships with others.

Ephesians 2:8-10 combines the subjects of how and why God saved us. While focusing upon the importance of the believer's good deeds, let us not forget that a person can be redeemed only by means of *something else.*

11 According to Ephesians 2:8, how can a person be saved?

....

Let us conclude this section by reemphasizing the following two points concerning the believer's works:

1. Man is not forgiven or saved through his works. It is only through his faith in what Jesus Christ did for him on the cross. The death of Christ paid the price for man's sinfulness. Now man can be saved through God's grace. This grace is undeserved, free love and mercy upon us.

2. Although works do not save the sinner, or redeem the believer, they are, nonetheless, the purpose or goal of the Christian life. We are born with a purpose: to glorify the Father through useful lives.

Continuing by the Holy Spirit

Objective 5. *Explain how the Holy Spirit wants to relate us to Christ through character and works.*

The Holy Spirit gives the believer life. The believer must learn to let the Holy Spirit control his life. Much of our study has concerned this. The evidence of the Holy Spirit's control of our personality is Christ's character in us. But the evidence of the Holy Spirit's control over our mind and will is works—works which continue Christ's ministry and glorify the Father.

The gifts of the Holy Spirit are special abilities given the believer to do the will of God. Romans 12 and 1 Corinthians 12 are important places of teaching concerning these special abilities. Romans 12:5-6 tells us that:

> Though we are many, we are one body in union with Christ, and we are all joined to each other as different parts of one body. So we are to use our different gifts in accordance with the grace that God has given us.

Different functions of the members of our physical body illustrate well the different spiritual ministries of believers. The fingers must be able to do specific tasks. They must be able to hold tools. Your fingers *must control the pencil* you use in this course. But the toes are not like the fingers. Very few people could use their toes like their fingers! Yet, the toes help us hold our balance, walk, run, and so forth.

12 Now, read Romans 12:6-8. I can count seven different ministries for believers. See if you can find them and list them here. (I have listed the first two for you).

a Speak God's message   e ....

b Serve   f ....

c .... g ....

d ....

The passage in 1 Corinthians 12 is the most studied Scripture concerning *gifts* from the Holy Spirit. We are told here that:

> There are different kinds of spiritual gifts but the same Spirit gives them. There are different ways of serving, but the same Lord is served. There are different abilities to perform service, but the same God gives ability to everyone for their particular service. The Spirit's presence is shown in some way in each person for the good of all (1 Corinthians 12:4-7).

13 What follows in 1 Corinthians 12:8-11 is a listing of nine special abilities or gifts. Three of these gifts have to do with speaking. We call them speech or utterance gifts. Separate them from the others and list them:

a ....

b ....

c ....

Another three gifts in this passage have to do with unusual scriptural spiritual power. These are: (1) the power of special faith, (2) the power to heal, and (3) the power to work miracles. You can see that these special powers enable the believer to do many of the wonderful works which Jesus did.

The last three gifts listed in 1 Corinthians 12:8-11 have to do with · special abilities to think and understand above the human level. These are (1) a message full of wisdom, (2) a message full of knowledge, and (3) the ability to tell the difference between gifts that come from the Spirit and those that do not.

Each one of these special abilities makes it possible for believers to do special works which show the likeness of Jesus Christ. These gifts are always to draw attention to Jesus, not to the person through whom they operate. An entire chapter in the Bible, 1 Corinthians 14, tells us how these gifts are to function. A good reminder for us is found in 1 Corinthians 14:12: "Since you are eager to have the gifts of the Spirit, you must try above everything else to make greater use of those which help to build up the church."

14 As believers, we must submit our lives to the Holy Spirit's control so that he can change our character and works according to His desire. How does the Spirit want to relate us to Christ through character and works?

....

SUMMARY

Jesus once told a story about work (see Matthew 21:28-31). It involved two sons. The father asked the older son, "Son, go and work in the vineyard today." "I don't want to," he answered, but later changed his mind and went. Then the father went to the other son and said the same thing. "Yes, sir," he answered, but he did not go. Then Jesus asked those who were listening, "Which one of the two did what his father wanted?" The people who were listening said, "The elder one." The message in that story is clear. It is *doing* the will of God that counts—not talking about it. A powerful evidence of Christian maturity is a life of usefulness.

15 In Matthew 25:34-36, Jesus mentions six good works that righteous people have done. Read this passage and list those works here. (I have given the first one to you.)

a Feed the hungry.

b ....

c ....

d ....

e ....

f ....

It is important to notice that Jesus informed the righteous that good works that they had done for needy people were counted as having been done for Him (Matthew 25:37-40).

There are many such Scriptures that we could study. Our purpose, however, is simply to understand that usefulness in our Christian life is an evidence of Christian maturity. "Your light must shine before people," Jesus said, "so that they will see the good things you do and praise your Father in heaven" (Matthew 5:16).

self-test

TRUE-FALSE. Write **T** in the blank space if the statement is true. Write **F** if it is false.

... **1** God wanted man to have power over the fish, the birds, and the animals.

... **2** The witness of John the Baptist was a greater witness to Jesus than the deeds that Jesus Himself did.

... **3** The gifts of the Holy Spirit enable the believer to produce works like those of Jesus Christ in his life.

SHORT ANSWER. Write in the proper answers to the questions on the lines provided.

4 What idea does the phrase "fully qualified and equipped" express?

....

....

According to 1 Corinthians 12:8-11, what are the three special gifts of the Holy Spirit which give Christians supernatural ability in speaking?

5 ....

6 ....

7 ....

List three of the six good works for which Jesus commended righteous people in Matthew 25:34-36.

8 ....

9 ....

10 ....

answers to the study questions

1 c) Jesus' works.

9 By doing useful work for the church.

2 a While it is day.
  b The night.

10 c) That the believer's life will produce good deeds.

3 The things He did by the Father's authority.

11 By God's grace through faith.

4 Because the Father had given Him His work.

12 a See example.
   b See example.
   c Teach.
   d Encourage others.
   e Share with others.
   f Use authority.
   g Show kindness.

5 By Christian believers.

13 a Speaking God's message.
   b Speech in strange tongues.
   c Explanation of speech in strange tongues.

6 He must remain in Jesus and Jesus' words must remain in him.

14 The Spirit wants to form the character of Christ in us and show
   the works of Christ through us.

7 Obey Jesus' commands.

15 a (Example)
   b Give drink to the thirsty.
   c Receive the stranger.
   d Clothe the naked.
   e Take care of the sick.
   f Visit those in prison.

8 the Holy Spirit, wisdom.

for your notes

Lesson 10

Evidence of Spiritual Transformation

I'm sure you're glad to be near the end of this course. There is always a feeling of joy when we finish something important. I have enjoyed leading you through this study. It has been a journey which has taken us through much of the Bible. Christian maturity is a subject very close to God's heart.

Together we have studied pictures of Christian maturity, progress in Christian maturity and, finally, proofs of Christian maturity. This last unit has given us a measuring rod to help us determine our progress. Those who are maturing as believers will begin to look and act like Jesus Christ. They will have more and more of His character and His works in their lives.

Perhaps you are a bit discouraged when you see the goal. It seems so difficult. We are but human beings. To measure ourselves by the standard which Jesus Christ achieved in His life upon this earth seems hard. Cheer up! God not only sets the standard for us, He helps us reach the goal. It is God's greatest delight to take weak people and show His power of transformation through them. This is the great hope of our calling in Jesus Christ.

lesson outline

Strength in Weakness
    God's Glory
    God's Power
Doubt and Condemnation of Self
    Doubting Our Ability
    Doubt Caused by Satan's Accusations
Transformation Through the Holy Spirit

lesson objectives

When you finish this lesson you should be able to:

■ Explain how God's glory is seen through man's weakness.

■ Use specific examples to describe results of God's transforming power in men.

learning activities

1. Read the lesson in this textbook.

2. Do the exercises in the lesson development, referring as needed to the textbook. Check your answers periodically with those given in the textbook.

3. Take the self-test at the end of this lesson, and check your answers carefully. Review those items answered incorrectly.

key words

accusation
achieved
attitude
boast

condemnation
record
specific

---

lesson development

STRENGTH IN WEAKNESS

Objective 1: *Identify the believer's sources of strength and weakness.*

People who study birds tell us that they fly much higher when moving to a distant place than when in local flight. We are told that there are three reasons for this higher flight. First, by flying higher they have a better view and more easily find their direction. Second, they are above the birds which would prey upon them. Third, thinner air at a higher level helps them fly faster. All of these reasons help birds to reach distant goals.

The believer can learn a lesson from this. When he is filled with doubts, he looks at life from such a low level that he cannot see his way, and Satan tempts him. It is only when he rises to the purer air of God's view of his life that he receives spiritual sight and strength to reach God's goal for him.

Perhaps you are already saying, "I don't believe I can ever achieve spiritual maturity. I am so weak. How can I ever be like Jesus?" That very attitude can be a start in the right direction. When a person feels strong in his own abilities, he will tend to lean upon them. A believer who recognizes his weakness will be able to better realize his need to look to God for help.

1 Name the believer's sources of strength and weakness.

....

....

God's Glory

Objective 2: *Use 1 Corinthians 1:26-31 to point out what the believer is to boast of.*

We have seen that man apart from God tries to show his independence by rebellion and sin. He exalts human wisdom and depends on human strength. This is the story of every civilization. God chose Christ's sacrifice and faith as the means of right standing with Him. This insulted the world's thinking.

In I Corinthians 1:21 Paul calls the message of the gospel a "so called 'foolish' message." It is a message of dependence upon God. The world rejects this. The truth of this message has an important relationship to this study. Here, we present a very important passage of Scripture on this subject. Read it carefully:

> Now remember what you were, my brothers, when God called you. From the human point of view few of you were wise or powerful or of high social standing. God purposely chose what the world considers nonsense in order to shame the wise, and he chose what the world considers weak in order to shame the powerful. He chose what the world looks down on and despises, and thinks is nothing, in order to destroy what the world thinks is important. This means that no one can boast in God's presence. But God has brought you into union with Christ Jesus, and God has made Christ to be our wisdom. By him we are put right with God; we become God's holy people and are set free. So then, as the scripture says, "Whoever wants to boast must boast of what the Lord has done" (1 Corinthians 1:26-31).

2 According to 1 Corinthians 1:26-31, the believer's wisdom is to be
a) Christ Jesus.
b) the Bible.
c) his mental growth.

3 According to 1 Corinthians 1:26-31, what is the believer to boast of?

....

God desires that man will glorify Him—not the instrument He uses. That is hard to do when the instrument is strong or beautiful. This should encourage most of us because we know we cannot do anything in ourselves. Thus, God finds a great opportunity to reveal His glory through us.

The life of the apostle Paul is an example of God's revelation of His glory through human weakness. Although well educated, Paul had many pressing weaknesses. One of them was a painful physical ailment which he asked God to remove (2 Corinthians 12:7-8). God once told him: "My grace is all you need, for my power is strongest when you are weak" (2 Corinthians 12:9). The apostle then wrote:

> I am most happy, then, to be proud of my weaknesses, in order to feel the protection of Christ's power over me. I am content with weaknesses, insults, hardships, persecutions, and difficulties for Christ's sake. For when I am weak, then I am strong (2 Corinthians 12:9-10).

God makes us so that we may glorify Him. Let us try to glorify the Lord in all we do and say.

God's Power

Objective 3: *Use Ezekiel 2:2 to explain what enabled Ezekiel to stand on his feet before God.*

Another example of God's revelation of His power through human weakness is the Old Testament prophet Ezekiel. He was a thirty-year-old priest when God called him. His nation was defeated and being destroyed. The very purpose of his own life (the priesthood) was almost useless. He was working as a captive on a farm. In Ezekiel chapters 1-2 we read about the call of God to him in these circumstances. It came in the midst of a terrible storm (Ezekiel 1:4). This must have represented the very confusion Ezekiel felt in his life. God revealed His power in this storm. Let us read Ezekiel's own description in Ezekiel 2:1-3:

> When I saw this, I fell face downwards on the ground. Then I heard a voice saying, "Mortal man, stand up. I want to talk to

you." While the voice was speaking, God's Spirit entered me and raised me to my feet, and I heard the voice continue, "Mortal man, I am sending you to the people of Israel."

The name God used for Ezekiel, *Mortal man* or *Son of man,* is very interesting. It is a strong word which draws attention to Ezekiel's humanity. The name appears very frequently in the book of Ezekiel. God is constantly reminding Ezekiel that He wants to work through his humanity. The name *Ezekiel* means, "the one whom God will strengthen" or "he whose character is personal proof of the strengthening of God." Today, we would describe such a person by saying: "If that man ever does anything good the people will know that it had to be God!" Ezekiel is a helpful example to us through both his name and his actions.

4 Read Ezekiel 2:2 and answer the following question: How was Ezekiel able to stand upon his feet before God?
a) Ezekiel got up through his own power.
b) God's command itself raised Ezekiel.
c) God's Spirit entered Ezekiel and raised him up.

The personality of Ezekiel was transformed by God's power. It was through that transforming power alone that the former weak and confused Ezekiel could affirm: "I did what the Lord told me to do" (Ezekiel 12:7). God received the glory from his long and fruitful ministry.

DOUBT AND CONDEMNATION OF SELF

Many of the people God has called to serve Him have felt unable to do it. Such a feeling in itself is not wrong. But sometimes that feeling is a lack of faith in the God who has made us. Such a condition sometimes leads a weak Christian to condemn himself (that is, declare himself guilty). God knows our weaknesses. *When He chooses us He gives us the strength and power to do His calling.* If we allow doubt and condemnation of self to keep us from fulfilling God's purpose, we lack faith in Him.

Doubting Our Ability

Objective 4: *List four things that Timothy was told to practice so that his progress could be seen by all.*

In Exodus 3, we read that God called Moses to serve Him. Moses doubted that he was able to serve God. When God miraculously spoke to him from the burning bush, Moses answered, "Yes, here I am" (verse 4). God told Moses that He was sending him to the king of Egypt so that he could lead His people out of the country. But Moses immediately answered, "I am nobody. How can I go to the king and bring the Israelites out of Egypt?" (verse 11). God said, "I will be with you, and when you bring the people out of Egypt, you will worship me on this mountain. That will be the proof that I have sent you" (verse 12). Then, Moses made a series of excuses: "What can I tell them?" (verse 13). "Suppose the Israelites do not believe me" (Exodus 4:1). And finally, "No, Lord, don't send me. I have never been a good speaker, and I haven't become one since you began to speak to me. I am a poor speaker, slow and hesitant" (verse 10). The Lord said to him, "Who gives man his mouth? Who makes him deaf or dumb? Who gives him sight or makes him blind? It is I, the Lord. Now go! I will help you to speak, and I will tell you what to say" (verses 11-12). But Moses said, 'No, Lord, please send someone else" (verse 13). At this point, the Lord became angry with Moses.

It is interesting to note God's patience in this story about Moses. God understood his doubt and was willing to work with every issue. However, when Moses continued to argue with God, it became an issue of lack of faith. Finally, Moses did go to Egypt and each day his confidence grew as God helped him. He became a great leader for God.

Perhaps during this course you have begun to realize your purpose as a believer. There is a high call from God upon your life. The goal of Christian maturity seems difficult. As you grow in God you realize there will be more duties. You might even doubt your ability as Moses did, but when God calls us He promises to help. God made every part of us. He knows us better than we know ourselves. *We must overcome our own inability through exercise of faith in God.* He is a God of power and His glory is shown as He uses weak persons to do great work.

5 Read 1 Timothy 4:11-16. According to verse 12, Timothy was advised not to let anyone look down on him because he was
a) not handsome.
b) young.
c) weak.

6 There are four things which Timothy was told in 1 Timothy 4:13-15 to practice so that his progress could be seen by all. List them in the order they are mentioned.

a ....

b ....

c ....

d ....

Doubt Caused by Satan's Accusations

Objective 5: *Identify a major source of doubts and state how you can overcome them.*

Many times Satan influences us to doubt ourselves. He is, as we have seen, the opposer of the believer. He works to bring the believer into confusion. He accuses and points out weaknesses. Some Christians become discouraged under Satan's attacks. They believe his lies. What he tells them confirms their own feelings about themselves, and they condemn themselves.

After 70 years in captivity, God made it possible for his people to go back home to Jerusalem. Joshua was chosen to be the spiritual leader. He was the high priest. (Don't confuse this Joshua with the Joshua who first brought the people into the promised land.) When God's people got back to Jerusalem, they immediately started to rebuild the temple. That was good news! They soon became discouraged, however. There was opposition and grumbling. After the foundation was laid, the people gave up the work for 16 years! Finally God raised up the prophets Haggai and Zechariah to get the people moving again. In a special vision, God told Zechariah what one of the major problems was.

7 Read Zechariah chapter 3. Who stood ready to bring an accusation against Joshua?

....

8 Read Zechariah 3:3 again. What was there about Joshua that Satan could accuse him of?

....

The filthy clothes that Zechariah saw on Joshua seem to represent the mistakes that Joshua and the people had made. Nevertheless, the angel of the Lord answered the charges of Satan: "May the Lord condemn you, Satan! May the Lord, who loves Jerusalem, condemn you. This man is like a stick snatched from the fire" (Zechariah 3:2). Verses 4-5 tell us that the dirty robes were taken away. New clothes were given Joshua to wear. These included a turban which was a symbol of authority with God. In verses 6-7, Joshua is told to walk in a new relationship with the Lord. Then the last verses in this chapter tell of God's blessing upon that relationship.

This Scripture reveals to us how Satan works upon our weaknesses. He calls them to our attention. He accuses us. This causes us to doubt ourselves and become discouraged. Many times believers just simply give up. Notice, however, that God had the dirty robes taken off and the clean ones put on. *God will take care of our weaknesses and doubts when we stop listening to the accusation of Satan.*

What Satan does in accusing believers is called *condemnation.* *Condemnation* means "to declare someone unfit or unworthy," or "to judge and pronounce someone guilty." Romans 8:1 clearly tells us "There is no condemnation now for those who live in union with Christ Jesus." John said "Whoever believes in the Son is not judged (condemned); but whoever does not believe has already been judged, because he has not believed in God's only Son" (John 3:18). Satan tries to judge us and get us to look at our weakness. In this way he keeps us from victory. God will transform our personalities by His divine power if we will but let Him do it.

One of the pictures the Bible gives us of God's final victory over Satan is in Revelation 12:10-11. In this passage we find these important words:

Now God's salvation has come! Now God has shown his power as King! Now his Messiah has shown his authority! For the one who stood before our God and accused our brothers day and night has been thrown out of heaven. Our brothers won the victory over him by the blood of the Lamb and by the truth which they proclaimed; and they were willing to give up their lives and die.

9 Use a pencil to mark a (1), (2), and (3) in front of the three things in Revelation 12:11 (above) that brought the believers victory over Satan.

These three powers are available to us today. Remember the truth of the Scripture, "The Spirit who is in you is more powerful than the spirit in those who belong to the world" (1 John 4:4).

TRANSFORMATION THROUGH THE HOLY SPIRIT

Objective 6: *Explain how Acts 17:6 shows believers were spiritually transformed.*

The Bible is such an encouragement to us. Most of the men whom God chose to work through were much like us. Moses, Joshua, Ezekiel, Paul, Timothy, and many others were among them. They were very human and had normal weaknesses, but God's Spirit entered them and transformed them. The book of Acts tells of such transformation. The disciples were scattered and discouraged at the crucifixion of Jesus. Even the resurrection did not solve their problem. But when the Holy Spirit came upon them as Jesus promised, things changed. They worked and witnessed with great power.

10 Read John 14:26. Jesus told his disciples that the Father would send the Holy Spirit. What did Jesus call the Holy Spirit?
a) The Helper
b) The Healer
c) The Power

In Acts 1:8, Jesus told the disciples, "When the Holy Spirit comes upon you, you will be filled with power, and you will be witnesses for me in Jerusalem, in all Judaea and Samaria, and to the ends of the earth." The book of Acts records the story of transformed men. The disciples were simple men. They did not have great formal training. They were men with their own specific weaknesses. Yet, under the power of the Holy Spirit they "turned the world upside down." They were strong even while suffering and facing death.

11 "These that have turned the world upside down are come hither also" (Acts 17:6, KJV) was said of believers who were being helped by the Holy Spirit. How does this quotation from Scripture show these believers were spiritually transformed?

....

We have the same opportunity to bear witness to Jesus Christ through the power of the divine Helper. We know the goal of our Christian life, but we are too weak to reach it by our own strength. When we are weak, God can become strong in us. His Spirit can cause us to stand on our own feet. His Spirit can enable us to do the task He sends us to do. His Spirit places the nature of God within us. That nature is moving us toward the goal of Christlikeness. That goal is true Christian maturity.

self-test

SHORT ANSWER. Write in the proper answer to the question on the lines provided.

1 What is the advantage of viewing our lives as God views them?

....

TRUE-FALSE. Write **T** in the blank space if the statement is true. Write **F** if it is false. Then, change the **FALSE** statements to make them true.

... 2 The believer is supposed to boast of what the Lord has done.

The believer is supposed to boast of ....

... 3 Moses protested to God that he was a poor speaker.

Moses protested to God that he was ....

... 4 Condemnation means to declare someone fit and worthy. It is to judge someone innocent.

Condemnation means to declare someone .... and

....

It is to judge someone ....

MATCHING. Below you will find several illustrations of the basic concepts in this lesson. Match each illustration (5-9) to the concept it fits best (a-e) by writing the correct number in the blank before the concept.

5 The apostle Paul had weaknesses, including a painful physical ailment which he asked God to remove, but he was a powerful Christian worker.

6 God called Ezekiel "Mortal Man" very frequently in the book bearing Ezekiel's name.

7 Although the Lord listened patiently to Moses' excuses, He became angry when Moses continued to resist His plan for him.

8 Timothy was a young man who was advised not to allow people to reject him because of his youth.

9 Satan stood ready to accuse Joshua (the High Priest during Israel's restoration) when Joshua was shown in dirty robes before the angel of the Lord.

. . . a) God understands our weaknesses but He expects us to do His will by faith in His power.

. . . b) God wants to remind us of our humanity that we might depend upon His power.

. . . c) Satan tries to bring the believer into condemnation because of the believer's failure.

. . . d) The shortness of a believer's spiritual experience should not keep him from being an accepted example to other believers.

. . . e) God's power is strongest when the believer is weak.

MULTIPLE CHOICE. There is only one correct answer for the following question. Circle the letter of the correct answer.

10 Satan stands before God and works against the brethren as
a) a false reporter.
b) an accuser.
c) a common serpent.
d) a false prophet.

Be sure to complete your unit student report for Unit 3 and return the answer sheet to your ICI instructor.

---

answers to the study questions

1 God is the source of strength, and human beings are the source of weakness.

7 Satan.

2 a) Christ Jesus.

8 He was wearing filthy clothes.

3 Of what the Lord has done.

9 1) The blood of the Lamb.
2) The truth which they proclaimed.
3) Their willingness to give up their lives and die.

4 c) God's Spirit entered Ezekiel and raised him.

10 a) The Helper.

5 b) young.

11 This quotation shows that these believers were spiritually transformed through the Holy Spirit.

6 a Public reading of Scriptures.
b Preaching.
c Teaching.
d Not neglecting the spiritual gift within him.

Glossary

The right-hand column lists the lesson in the independent study textbook in which the word is used.

accusation	— wrong saying against someone	10
achieved	— gained; finished successfully	3,10
adulterous	— referring to sexual unfaithfulness	2
architect	— man who makes plans for a new building	3
artisan	— skilled workman	3
attitude	— way in which one feels or thinks about something	3,10
audience	— hearers, people in a meeting	6
automatic	— moving or working by itself	4
boast	— speak proudly of	10
brokenness	— weakened in strength or spirit; tamed, crushed	3
character	— one's nature as shown by one's acts	8
childish	— like a child	3
commend	— praise	9
condemnation	— declaration of unfitness	10
conformed	— be like; make similar	3
conviction	— what one believes to be right	3
cultivate	— prepare (land) for crops	3,9
cycle	— set of events regularly repeated in a particular order	5
destiny	— fate	1

direction	— a specific instruction	6
doctrine	— what is taught	7
dynamic	— having to do with or producing power or force	1
enable	— make able	8,9
endeavor	— attempt	5
equip	— supply with the necessary knowledge for doing certain special work	5
equipped	— supplied with the necessary knowledge for doing certain special work	9
evaluation	— fixing of the value of	1
eventual	— coming in the end	5
excellent	— very good	6
fellowship	— companionship, friendliness; sharing	1
foundation	— the basis	3,7
glorify	— praise highly	1,9
growth	— act or amount of growing	1
grow up	— (of a person) become older	6
guarantee	— promise to see that another person fulfills his promise	7
hinder	— effort to stop someone or something	4
hindrance	— anything that causes trouble or difficulty	4
homosexual	— one who enjoys sexual relations with persons of the same sex	2
image	— likeness or copy of anything	2
interact	— have an effect upon each other	6
intimate	— inside, close	8

issue	— matter on which a decision must be reached	5
judicial	— having to do with a judge	5
knowledge	— things known	8
lens	— piece of glass which collects light into one beam	6
liken	— compare	5
manifestation	— showing	8
maturity	— state of being fully grown	1
negligence	— failure to exercise care	4
observe	— act according to, notice	8
obvious	— clearly noticed	6
option	— which may or may not be done, at one's own choice	5
ordain	— officially appoint or consecrate as a minister in a Christian church	7
paralyzed	— made unable to move	9
penance	— suffering given to oneself as a sign of sorrow for wrongdoing	7
perfect	— complete or whole	1
preparatory	— getting ready	5
prevail	— win, become generally accepted as a custom	6
purpose	— aim, desire, plan	1
qualification	— a quality or skill that fits a person (as for an office)	9
rational	— reasonable	4

record	— set down in writing, or a setting down in writing	10
redeem	— save from the punishment of evil-doing	9
relationship	— state of being related, connection	1
remarkable	— worthy of notice, specially good	6
reminder	— something to remind someone of something	9
repentance	— to turn inwardly and outwardly away from something	3,7
require	— need	5,7
response	— answer	6
responsibility	— something for which one is responsible	3
resurrection	— rising again from the dead	7
sacred	— solemn	6
seek	— look for, try to get	5
sift	— examine very carefully	4
specific	— having to do with one particular thing	10
stature	— development; physical, mental or moral growth	1
tool	— person or thing used by another like a tool	6
ultimate	— last, final	1,5
victorious	— successful	8
viewpoint	— way of looking on or considering something	3
vital	— full of life and spirit, lively	6,7
weapon	— instrument used for fighting (or protection)	6

Answers to Self-Tests

SELF-TEST 1

1 F

2 F

3 T

4 F

5 T

6 a) Full grown.
   c) Complete.
   d) Whole.
   e) Finished.

7 c) spirit.

8 b) As a model of correct God-man relationship.
   c) That man might be brought into abundant life.

9 Satan.

10 *Any two of the following*: soil along the path, rocky ground without moisture, soil with choking thorns, good soil.

SELF-TEST 2

1 T

2 T

3 F, Jesus Christ.

4 a) Spiritual.
   b) Physical.
   d) Mental.
   h) Social.

5 a) Immoral.
   d) Adulterous.
   e) Homosexual.

6 b) That of a servant.

7 a Family (other than spouse).
   b Friends.
   c Husband or wife.
   d Neighbors.

SELF-TEST 3

1 When he becomes a mature believer.

2 a 2
   b 4
   c 3
   d 1

3 b) A baby.
   c) God's field.
   f) Soil.
   h) God's building.
   j) The temple of the Holy Spirit.

4 a) Gold.
   e) Silver.
   f) Precious stones.

SELF-TEST 4

1 F, a great deal to do with the believer's maturity.

2 T

3 F, grow slower than one who receives solid food.

4 F, spirit.

5 T

6 a) be teachers.

7 Any four of these nine: love, joy, peace, patience, kindness, goodness, faithfulness, humility, self-control.

SELF-TEST 5

1 F, moves us to action.
2 T
3 T
4 T
5 F, works (or life)
6 E
7 T
8 T
9 E
10 E
11 T
12 The judgment seat of Christ.

SELF-TEST 6

1-7 Your answers.
8 F
9 F
10 T
11 b) Fellowship, sharing, contributing.
12 Immaturity, lack of vital union and disease or impairment are three such causes (there are others).

SELF-TEST 7

1 F

2 T
3 T
4 F
5 F
6 T
7 F
8 Repentance.
9 Believing in God.
10 Baptisms.
11 Laying on of hands.
12 Resurrection of the dead.
13 Eternal judgment.

SELF-TEST 8

1 T
2 T
3 F
4 T
5 T
6 a) Goodness.
   c) Peace.
   f) Patience.
   g) Kindness.
   j) Faithfulness.
   k) Humility.
   l) Self-control.
   m) Love.
   o) Joy.
7 Your answer.

SELF-TEST 9

1 T
2 F
3 T

4 The idea of maturity.

5 Speaking God's message.

6 Speech in strange tongues.

7 Explanation of speech in strange tongues.

8-10 Any three of the following:
Feed the hungry.
Give drink to the thirsty.
Receive the stranger.
Clothe the naked.
Take care of the sick.
Visit those in prison.

SELF-TEST 10

1 Viewing our lives as God views them will enable us to reach God's goal for us.

2 T

3 T

4 F, unfit, unworthy, guilty

5-9 a) 7
    b) 6
    c) 9
    d) 8
    e) 5

10 b) an accuser.